I0479882

Empire of Influence

*Leadership Strategies Forged in
the Fires of Ancient Rome*

RODNEY D. REIDER

"What we do now echoes in eternity."

-Marcus Aurelius, *Meditations*

TENTHPOWERPUBLISHING
www.tenthpowerpublishing.com

Design by Inkwell Creative

Softcover ISBN 978-1-938840-68-5
e-book ISBN 978-1-938840-69-2

10 9 8 7 6 5 4 3 2 1

To those who aspire to be individuals of positive influence
and have chosen the path of leadership to make this impact
possible now, while establishing a legacy
for others to follow in the future.

Other Books by Rodney D. Reider

Grabbing the Next Rung: The Heart of Leadership

ABOUT THE AUTHOR

From the boardroom to the frontlines of modern healthcare, Dr. Rodney D. Reider has spent his career leading complex organizations, guiding innovation, and helping others navigate change with clarity and purpose. His professional journey spans every corner of the healthcare industry—from serving as CEO of billion-dollar systems, to advising startups and Private Equity ventures—giving him a rare 360-degree view of how leadership shapes lives at every level.

Rodney has worked closely with boards, physicians, employees, and communities to strengthen core services, improve performance, and foster strategic alliances. His leadership has helped position organizations to adapt and thrive in a rapidly evolving healthcare landscape.

A lifelong student of leadership and history, Rodney believes that timeless wisdom holds powerful lessons for today's challenges. His passion for Roman philosophy and systems-thinking helped inspire Empire of Influence, where ancient leadership principles meet modern-day executive realities. He has written and spoken extensively on leadership, culture, and resilience—always aiming to leave a lasting impact on the industries and individuals he serves.

Rodney holds multiple advanced degrees, including a Bachelor of Arts from Chapman University; an MBA from Loma Linda University; a Master of Science from California State Polytechnic University; and both a Master of Arts and a Doctorate from Harrison Middleton University. He has been named an International Scholar twice and is a Fellow of the American

College of Healthcare Executives.

An international speaker and thought leader, Rodney has had the honor of teaching, moderating, and delivering keynotes at conferences around the world—from New York City, to Tel Aviv. His leadership contributions have been recognized with multiple awards, including CEO of Influence by the State of Idaho and being named Honorary Commander of the Idaho National Guard.

When he's not decoding Roman strategy or helping leaders sharpen their edge, Rodney enjoys classic literature, adventurous travel, and occasionally losing debates to his cat. He continues to serve on numerous boards and foundations, always seeking to elevate the communities of which he is a member.

To learn more or get in touch, visit www.RodneyDReider.com.

TABLE OF CONTENTS

Part III Systems, Strategy, and Legacy

Appendix

"It is the power of the mind to be unconquerable."

—Seneca

INTRODUCTION

Why Rome? Why Now?
The Impact of Leadership
in Healthcare and Business

L eadership has always been the cornerstone of success, whether in healthcare, business, or beyond. Strong leadership can shape not only organizations but entire industries. In today's fast-paced and ever-changing world, leaders are not merely managing teams, they're influencing lives, shifting markets, and driving innovation. With the rapid pace of change, the right kind of leadership has never been more essential to survival and success.

Each chapter of this book explores how the foundational leadership lessons from ancient Rome remain surprisingly relevant today. Rome is the empire by which all other great societies are measured. It is no wonder that efforts to emulate and revive its legacy have echoed across the centuries. The Roman Empire was a powerhouse of strategy, innovation, and governance. It was led by some of the most remarkable leaders in history.

Entrepreneurs, healthcare executives, and modern business leaders can draw on these ancient insights to guide their organizations through complexity, uncertainty, and change. The past is meant to be studied. It is a powerful blueprint for building a successful future.

The viral question "How often do you think about the Roman Empire?" tends to elicit a surprisingly enthusiastic response from men of all ages. There is a reason an empire that officially fell in 476 AD still occupies the modern imagination. Admiration spans from the reputations of its visionary leaders to the might of the disciplined Roman legions. These legions, known for their order, ferocity, and battlefield dominance, represent more than brute strength; they symbolize discipline, endurance, and legacy.

Today we are still surrounded by Roman reminders: the massive aqueduct systems, durable underwater concrete, the Colosseum, the Roman Forum, and the Pantheon. These enduring structures, and the vision behind them, speak volumes about the innovation and order that defined Roman civilization.

For many of us, our first real connection to Rome was not through textbooks but through cinema. Older generations may remember the grandeur of *Ben-Hur*, while others were introduced to Roman ideals through Ridley Scott's *Gladiator*. This film continues to captivate audiences with its rich tapestry of leadership themes on honor, loyalty, power, betrayal, and justice. These demonstrated characteristics define the impact a single leader can have on the fate of many.

Characters in *Gladiator*

To kick off our exploration of Rome's leadership legacy, we begin with *Gladiator* (2000). Its complex characters offer rich insights into the qualities of influential leadership. Consider the following characters:

Maximus Decimus Meridius (played by Russell Crowe)

Maximus is a Roman general, wronged by the betrayal of Emperor Commodus. He stands firm for what is right, even when faced with overwhelming odds. Maximus's leadership style is rooted in loyalty, honor, and justice, most often leading by example. His men, on the field of battle or within the gladiatorial arena, love, admire, and respect him tremendously.

Maximus demonstrates what it means to lead with integrity, putting the needs of his men and the Roman Empire above his own desires.

Despite losing his family, his position, and his status, Maximus does not break. He continues to fight for justice, proving the power of perseverance.

His moral compass remains intact even as he faces betrayal and suffering, showing the importance of sticking to one's values. His ethical leadership is displayed throughout the film.

Leadership Traits: Integrity, Resilience, Strategic Thinking, Honor

Commodus (played by Joaquin Phoenix)

Commodus is the emperor who ascends to power by murdering his father, Marcus Aurelius, and then seeks to control Rome with cruelty and manipulation. His leadership is rooted in insecurity and a desperate need for validation, which leads to reckless decisions and ultimately his downfall. His vanity and desire for control come at the cost of Rome's well-being.

Commodus manipulates those around him to maintain power, including killing anyone who challenges his rule. This shows the destructive nature of leadership built on deceit and fear.

Commodus is shown to be a leader who lacks vision and integrity. He cannot inspire loyalty because he rules through intimidation rather than respect.

Leadership Traits: Self-interest, Vanity, Manipulation, Insecurity

Marcus Aurelius (played by Richard Harris)

Marcus Aurelius serves as the philosopher-king. Comparable to his historical representations, Emperor Marcus exudes wisdom and insight in his conversations. In the film, he also expresses a deep concern with the future of Rome and its ethical foundations. He wishes to return Rome to a republic, not ruled by a single emperor. Before his death, he entrusts Maximus with the future of the empire, knowing that his son Commodus is not fit for leadership.

Marcus Aurelius has a clear vision of what Rome should be, which is why he chooses to trust Maximus to lead rather than his own son. He prioritizes the good of the people over familial ties.

Marcus Aurelius understands the importance of legacy and makes his decisions with wisdom and foresight, which is key in strong leadership. He also values discernment and knowledge, as displayed in his philosophical nature.

His desire to make Rome a republic rather than an empire shows a commitment to ethical governance and serving the greater good.

Leadership Traits: Wisdom, Compassion, Visionary Leadership

Lucilla (played by Connie Nielsen)

Lucilla is Commodus's sister, who is torn between loyalty to her family and her desire to see Rome governed justly. She helps Maximus in his quest to avenge her father and stop her brother's tyrannical rule.

Lucilla's situation is a powerful study of leadership in which personal loyalties must sometimes be put aside for the greater good. She is loyal to her family but understands that Commodus is dangerous and must be stopped.

Lucilla uses her intelligence to navigate the dangerous political landscape of the palace. She helps Maximus not with brute force, but through subtlety and strategic alliances.

Lucilla is willing to take risks to help Maximus and do what is right, even though it puts her in danger.

Leadership Traits: Diplomacy, Intelligence, Moral Courage

Proximo (played by Oliver Reed)

Proximo is a former gladiator turned owner of a gladiatorial school. He becomes a mentor of sorts to Maximus in the arena, offering advice on survival and leadership in a brutal, unforgiving world.

Proximo teaches Maximus the importance of understanding, surviving, and even capitalizing on the system despite the depth of its corruption. Sometimes, to achieve a larger goal, leaders must make pragmatic choices.

Although he is a former gladiator who has learned to live by his wits, Proximo shows loyalty to Maximus and is willing to risk everything to help him achieve his goals. This highlights the importance of loyalty in leadership, even in difficult circumstances.

Proximo is a resourceful leader who knows how to navigate the difficult world of gladiatorial combat, using his understanding of the system to his advantage.

Leadership Traits: Pragmatism, Loyalty, Resourcefulness

Gracchus (played by Derek Jacobi)

Gracchus is a Roman senator who opposes Commodus' rule and seeks to return power to the Senate. He's a political strategist who works in the shadows to weaken Commodus' grip on power.

Gracchus understands the importance of working within the

system, even despite its corruption. He tries to bring about change through legal means rather than through violence, demonstrating the value of political acumen.

Despite the danger to himself, Gracchus remains dedicated to restoring the Senate's power and ensuring justice for Rome. His leadership shows the importance of standing up for what is right, even when it's not easy.

Gracchus is willing to face Commodus' wrath in order to support the greater good of the Roman people. He exemplifies moral courage in the political arena.

Leadership Traits: Courage, Political Savvy, Commitment to Justice

Juba (played by Djimon Hounsou)

Juba is a fellow gladiator who becomes Maximus's friend and ally. Juba's quiet strength and loyalty make him a valuable companion throughout Maximus's journey in the arena.

Juba exemplifies the power of loyalty and brotherhood in leadership. Even when facing death in the arena, he remains steadfast in his commitment to Maximus.

Juba's strength is more internal than external, as he is a calm, reflective character who demonstrates that leadership doesn't always have to be loud or forceful. Sometimes, it is about staying true to your values and your comrades.

Leadership Traits: Loyalty, Brotherhood, Inner Strength

These characters reveal how leadership, regardless of context, is about inspiring others, staying true to your principles, and having

the courage to make difficult decisions for the greater good.

And it begs the question: Could we do the same?

During *Gladiator,* Maximus suffers unimaginable loss and betrayal. Once a decorated general, he is stripped of his title, his family is murdered, and he is sold into slavery by the very empire he served with honor and courage. In one early scene, Maximus is tested in a brutal "interview" by his new master, forced to encounter a massive opponent while refusing to respond or show his strength. He endures the painful beating, never flinching nor defending himself. Yet even in defeat, his quiet strength commands attention. His future in the arena is sealed.

As modern leaders, we may not face Maximus's battlefield, but we *do* face circumstances that can feel just as crushing. We may feel pummeled by industry disruption, diminished by decisions beyond our control, or challenged to defend our values in environments that reward compromise. And yet, we endure. We lead. Because that is who we are.

We press on with our vision, even as external forces test our limits. We explain, advocate, and persist for our teams, our missions, and our communities. This is what defines us in the real-world arena of leadership.

We can certainly learn from fictional leaders. If you have not seen *Gladiator*, it is worth your time. But beyond the screen, the Roman Emperors, tasked with running a vast and complex empire, provide leadership lessons grounded in reality. Their lives, decisions, and challenges offer powerful and tangible insights.

We learn best when we are inspired and that positive inspiration can come from anywhere. The characters of *Gladiator* remind us that leadership is about persistence, principle, and purpose, not perfection.

Leadership Lessons from *Gladiator*

Integrity and Honor: Maximus teaches that a leader must stay true to their principles, even in the face of immense adversity.

Visionary Leadership: Marcus Aurelius and Gracchus highlight the importance of having a clear, long-term vision for the greater good of the people, not personal gain.

The Dangers of Ego and Power: Commodus's leadership is a cautionary tale about the dangers of insecurity, vanity, and ruling out of fear rather than respect.

Moral Courage: Characters such as Lucilla and Proximo show that sometimes the hardest part of leadership is making the right choice, even when it puts you at risk.

Loyalty and Brotherhood: Juba and Proximo exemplify quiet strength and deep trust. Inspiring loyalty and support through shared struggle and respect.

In the chapters ahead, we'll explore how Roman resilience, innovation, ethical leadership, and visionary thinking can empower you. As a leader today, you can build an empire of influence that endures far beyond your tenure.

"It is a rough road that leads to heights of greatness."

–Seneca

CHAPTER I

The Empire Within: Mastery before Mission

Focus: The internal foundation of leadership is self-awareness, discipline, and personal integrity. True empire-building starts within.

L et's go back to the beginning. You are competent. You have had a great deal of success. You have guided organizations through periods of change. And yet, you have felt the "punch in the stomach" over your career and some of its losses. Now, you must prove yourself again.

You interview for the position. You feel you do well, only to discover you are not the choice of the board or the oversight executive. You said all the right things. You answered every question with clarity and conviction; nevertheless, someone else was chosen. In many executive applicants' minds, this scenario has been repeated too frequently.

Why?

Or perhaps the question is better stated: "Is it really too often or does a portion of the additional preparation provide the impetus to better meet the challenge at the organization that truly needs your advanced skills the most?"

You interview again.

And again.

And again.

Once more, you feel good about the multiple conversations and discussions with potential peers, bosses, board members, and other important constituents, which are all part of the interview process. In addition, you do all your background research. The organization seems stable, though it faces obvious competitive and financial challenges. You accept the offer.

It is when you begin that the unveiling occurs. Deeper truths become apparent. The revealed strengths, weaknesses, and who you can rely on become clear and personally known. This is accelerated as the financial crisis becomes clearer. Now, the expertise gaps are more obvious, and the morale of the frontline is indelibly low. You are now in the midst of an organization hemorrhaging cash. Expense-side management becomes the immediate focus. Conscious consolidation, product line and service line reductions, and identifying any possible immediate growth opportunities become *the* primary focus. You search for truth in the "crises of survival." You are the leader of this organization. Are you adequately prepared?

Similar to Maximus' life suffering and betrayal, you have endured difficult experiences and faced many major challenges to gain the indispensable prior learnings for later application. As mentioned earlier, maybe not to the extent of Maximus' fall from serving the emperor and his victorious heights to becoming a lowly slave, forced to fight for the crowd's entertainment; nevertheless, perhaps now you begin to reflect on why you may have been forced to endure your own personal hardships. Was it part of the necessary and vital training in preparation to later conquer not only your own, but also the business challenges presently set before you? Was it any different for those who led in Rome during the Empire? A certain select group of humans, with all their foibles and personalities, are still called, or contain within them an utmost desire to thrive and be the leader.

What can we learn from the Roman leaders who chose to be, or found themselves, in charge? What was their decision-making style? Ultimately, how did they handle their crises? How will you handle yours? Is it just survival or time to thrive?

It does not matter the organization or time period, eventually a crisis will erupt. A company acquisition occurs with a dramatically different philosophy, advanced technology encroaches on the status quo, or existing economics are threatened with payments that fail to materialize. As historical leadership can show, sudden change can be confronted with a demonstration of resilience, strategic foresight, and adaptability. Now, the organization emerges even stronger from the leadership with an enhanced focus, clarity of vision, and the discipline necessary to achieve greater heights of accomplishment.

This chapter will illuminate the strategies employed by historical and modern leaders in order to avert disasters. Whether the challenge stems from pandemics, internal conflict, or external threats, generals and leaders throughout the ages have overcome. These leaders show that crises can be catapults for growth and resilience. You'll learn how to juggle the current demands with future obligations as well as maintain team morale and momentum in the midst of the dilemmas. Overall, it is essential to see that a challenge is not a catastrophe but a catalyst.

As leaders, we often enter the arena of Board meetings, leadership forums, and the many venues where we represent our organizations and employees. The authentic impact the Roman Emperors had on their world can also be translated to ours, but only through the positive influence that we as true leaders can bring.

The Empire Mindset: Leading with Purpose

Every successful leader knows that leadership is not exemplified by barking orders from the top; however, it is about envisioning the future and inspiring others to see it too. But let's be honest, it is not as if every day feels like a grand, visionary journey. There are moments when you feel more like you're managing chaos than building a legacy. During those situations, we can look to the ancient Romans for insight and advice.

One of the most compelling examples is Julius Caesar, who, at a crossroads of both opportunity and crisis, recognized the importance of setting bold visions. When Caesar crossed the Rubicon, a phrase that has since become a metaphor for making irreversible decisions, he demonstrated a fundamental truth for modern entrepreneurs: bold action defines leadership. In today's terms, Caesar did not *play it safe*; he staked everything on his vision and redefined the future of Rome.

As a business or healthcare leader, you may not be commanding armies or conquering new territories (though maybe you are!), but you are often faced with make-or-break decisions that can alter the course of your business. Just like Caesar, your ability to act decisively, take risks, and carry your team forward will define your legacy.

Yet, risk is not the only thing. Visionary leadership, as practiced by the likes of Caesar and Augustus, was built on the foundation of strategy and purpose. In today's entrepreneurial world, your vision must be equally strong and strategic. A great idea might light the fire, but a well-planned strategy fuels it long-term.

Rome was not built in a day, and neither are successful businesses (e.g., Starbucks, AirBnB, Netflix). Augustus, Caesar's successor, knew this well. After years of turmoil and civil war, Augustus did not merely rebuild Rome, he restructured its government, revitalized its economy, and set a long-term plan in place that secured peace for decades. His secret? The ability to blend *long-term vision with short-term execution.* Augustus was patient, yet decisive, slowly putting the right pieces into place to build an empire that would endure.

For leaders, this is a powerful lesson. It's tempting to constantly chase the "next big thing," but sustainable leadership requires a combination of patience, careful planning, and the ability to think far beyond the next quarter or fiscal year.

Leadership as the Act of Influence, Not Rigid Authority

For a moment, let's counter a common view. Too often, modern leadership is framed around power and authority: who's in charge, who's making decisions, who's got the final say. However, great leaders, demonstrated by those in Rome, understood that influence often outweighs authority. The most effective leaders swayed hearts and minds, rallied people to a shared cause, and created movements that transcended their own ambitions; they did not simply issue commands.

One figure who stands out is Marcus Aurelius, the Stoic philosopher-emperor. Despite holding the ultimate power in Rome, Marcus Aurelius understood that true leadership was about inspiring others to believe in something bigger than themselves. It was not about using force to make others follow. His personal journal, now known as *Meditations*, is a treasure trove of reflections on humility, self-discipline, and empathy.

In the space of encouragement and direction, leadership means guiding a team through the unknowns of innovation, pivoting through market shifts, and building a company culture that inspires loyalty and commitment. It must be about *influence over authority*, creating an environment where people feel empowered to take ownership, create, and take calculated risks. Your role is not for isolated directing; it is to inspire, shape, and empower!

Marcus Aurelius also teaches us that leadership is about resilience and balance. Running a business is not for the faint of heart, and neither is leading in healthcare. The challenges can seem overwhelming, regulatory pressures, operational complexities, and financial constraints. Yet leaders who embrace resilience will weather these storms with grace. By adopting a mindset that combines strategic foresight with personal discipline, as Aurelius did, today's leaders can remain calm in the face of uncertainty and lead by example.

Building Systems that Endure: Lessons from Roman Infrastructure

A strong leader is a builder of teams and an architect of systems that last. One of Rome's most enduring legacies is its infrastructure. The Roman aqueducts, roads, and public buildings were marvels of engineering, many of which remain today. This is not merely a historical footnote; it serves as a reminder that *lasting success requires building something that endures.*

Consider Rome's aqueduct system, which was constructed to bring water to the city from distant sources. The infrastructure was designed with strength and longevity, ensuring that future generations would benefit from the foresight and planning of its leaders.

As a business leader or healthcare executive, your responsibility is similar. You are not only managing the present, you also have the ultimate responsibility for building the future. It's easy to focus on quarterly earnings or immediate goals, but truly successful leaders think long-term. Whether it's creating robust operational systems, fostering a resilient company culture, or planning for succession, leaders must ensure that their vision extends beyond their immediate tenure.

Sustainability is the key concept here. Certain leaders, particularly in today's volatile markets, can be guilty of chasing rapid growth at the expense of building a sustainable foundation. But as Rome teaches us, long-term systems are what hold an empire, or a business, together.

Modern Business Leadership: Drawing from Roman Discipline

Let's return to the Roman army for a moment. The Roman military was known for its *discipline and precision*, and these same values are essential for modern business leaders. Just as Roman generals meticulously planned their campaigns, successful business leaders must ensure that their strategies are well thought out, their teams are well-prepared, and their execution is flawless.

In today's world of disruption and volatility, entrepreneurs and executives often face the temptation to improvise, pivot, or act on instinct. And while adaptability is crucial, a disciplined approach to leadership ensures that decisions are grounded in strategy, not just in reaction.

Rome teaches us that order is not a constraint; in fact, true discipline is liberating. Freedom within structure is a key foundational element of a high-performing organization or even an empire. It creates the ability to innovate, take risks, and explore new opportunities, knowing that you have a stable foundation to fall back on. A disciplined leader fosters a culture where expectations are clear, accountability is established, and excellence becomes a habit.

Special Section for Healthcare Executives: Competing Priorities

Healthcare executives, perhaps more than anyone else, must balance competing priorities: patient outcomes, operational efficiency, regulatory compliance, and financial performance. The leadership lessons from ancient Rome are especially relevant here, as healthcare leaders must blend *long-term vision, strategic foresight, and ethical decision-making* to succeed in an increasingly complex and regulated environment.

Strategic Vision for Healthcare Systems: Just as Augustus focused on long-term stability, healthcare executives need to craft a strategic vision that anticipates changes in patient care, technology, and policy. The healthcare industry is shifting rapidly with the rise of digital health, AI, telemedicine, and value-based care models. Leaders who think long-term and invest in scalable, sustainable systems will position their organizations for success in the decades ahead.

Ethical Leadership in Healthcare: Healthcare, by its very nature, involves life-and-death decisions. Ethical leadership is a mandate, not an option. Drawing from historical figures such as Marcus Aurelius and Cincinnatus, who utilized their powerful leadership position for the benefit of others, demonstrating personal accountability, and being able to walk away when the leadership mission is accomplished, is the optimal example for any leader. In healthcare, executives must do the same by being accountable for the benefit of others and placing patient well-being at the center of every decision. This means fostering a culture of *transparency, accountability, and integrity.* When facing difficult trade-offs, between cost containment and patient care, for instance, leaders must prioritize ethical considerations and maintain the trust of their patients and staff.

Resilience in Crisis Management: Healthcare leaders regularly face crises, whether from pandemics, resource shortages, or operational disruptions. Marcus Aurelius's Stoic resilience offers a guiding principle here: stay calm, focus on what you can control, and make rational, ethical decisions under pressure. The ability to remain steady, make clear decisions, and communicate effectively during crises is what distinguishes great healthcare leaders.

Building Sustainable Healthcare Models: Just as the Roman aqueducts ensured long-term water supply for the empire, healthcare executives must build systems that provide consistent, equitable care to diverse populations. This requires not only investment in infrastructure but also in people, nurturing talent, promoting wellness among healthcare providers, and designing systems that adapt to changing healthcare needs.

Reflection Questions

1. *Vision and Strategy:*
   How does your current leadership style reflect a balance between long-term vision and short-term execution? What steps can you take to ensure your decisions today are aligned with your future goals?

2. *Ethics and Integrity:*
   Reflect on a time when you had to make a difficult decision as a leader. How did ethical considerations guide your decision-making? Are there areas where you

can improve transparency or accountability in your leadership?

3. *Resilience and Discipline:*
   When faced with unexpected challenges, how do you maintain resilience? Are there practices, such as strategic planning or self-discipline, that you could implement to improve your ability to lead through uncertainty?

4. *System Building:*
   What infrastructure, whether technological, organizational, or cultural, are you building in your company or healthcare system that will endure?

   How can you ensure that the systems you build today will continue to provide value in the future? Ultimately, what structural legacy are you building to leave behind for others?

5. *Collaboration and Influence:*
   How do you inspire and influence your team or organization, rather than relying on authority? What steps can you take to foster a more collaborative and innovative work environment?

Final Thoughts: Timeless Strategies for Impact

By weaving together ancient wisdom with modern leadership principles, this chapter sets the stage for understanding how timeless strategies can influence today's entrepreneurial and healthcare landscapes. Leadership, whether in ancient Rome or a 21st-century boardroom, is about foresight, strategy, and the ability to inspire others to believe in a shared vision for the future.

Obiter Dictum:

In the most challenging seasons of my leadership career, I realized that self-discipline was what carried me. The organizational strategy is always a priority; however, getting up early, being focused, staying informed (listening), and preparing myself first gave me the footing to lead others and overcommunicate with clarity and confidence.

Scenario:

You step into a new leadership role and discover discontent and dysfunction beneath the polished exterior.

What Would a Worthy Roman Imperator Do?

Following Marcus Aurelius, you would first master yourself. Calm the internal storm before leading others. Self-discipline, quiet reflection, and decisive preparation forge the leadership empire you are about to build.

As every empire begins with inner discipline, so too must every grand vision start with clarity of purpose. With our internal compass calibrated, we now turn outward, toward those who dared to envision greatness not just for their time, but for all time.

*"A man's worth is no greater than
the worth of his ambitions."*

– Marcus Aurelius

CHAPTER II

Eyes on Eternity: Augustus and the Architecture of Vision

*Focus: Visionary leadership means building for generations,
not solely quarterly wins. This chapter explores how long-
term thinking forges empires that outlast their creators.*

Visionary leaders are not merely reactionary; they anticipate the future and shape it. In today's dynamic world, whether you're an entrepreneur launching the next big startup or a healthcare executive navigating the complexities of the system, the ability to see beyond the immediate challenges and forecast future needs is critical.

This chapter explores how visionary leaders throughout history, particularly in ancient Rome, transformed the systems around them by seeing what others could not. We'll draw lessons from great visionaries who shaped their fields, offering insights for entrepreneurs and executives seeking to lead their organizations into the future.

Vision Beyond the Horizon: Rome's Legacy of Bold Leadership

Let's start with a bold truth: Leadership is about seeing the future before anyone else can. The accountability for managing people and overseeing operations is inherent in the role; nevertheless, the most successful leaders, both in ancient Rome and today, are those who possess foresight, creativity, and the courage to act on their vision.

In Rome, no one embodied this better than Julius Caesar and Augustus. These men shattered the status quo, completely reshaping the very world in which they lived. Caesar, famous for his military exploits and role in transforming the Roman Republic into the Roman Empire, had an uncanny ability to anticipate political and military shifts long before his peers. Augustus, his successor, envisioned a Rome that would not only survive but thrive for centuries to come. He laid the groundwork for what would become the Pax Romana, a 200-year period of relative peace and prosperity.

These leaders understood a crucial truth: success lies not merely in responding to the present but ultimately in preparing for the future.

Case Study I: Julius Caesar and the Power of Visionary Risk-Taking

Julius Caesar's crossing of the Rubicon River in 49 BC is one of the most famous moments in Roman history. At the time, the Roman Senate had declared that any general who crossed the Rubicon with his army would be committing an act of war against Rome itself. Caesar's bold decision to cross the river was not a spur-of-the-moment act; it was a calculated risk, born from his vision of a stronger, more unified Rome.

Before making that fateful decision, Caesar recognized that the Roman Republic was crumbling under the weight of internal divisions and power struggles. He saw an opportunity to reshape the political landscape, even if it meant defying the Senate. His ultimate goal was to bring about long-term stability and order, and he was willing to take extraordinary risks to achieve that vision.

Empire of Influence Takeaway:

Caesar's actions serve as a powerful reminder for today's leaders and entrepreneurs: sometimes, you have to take bold risks to realize your vision. This doesn't mean acting recklessly, but rather taking calculated risks that others might shy away from. Visionary leaders look beyond the immediate consequences and focus on the bigger picture.

In business, this could mean betting on an emerging technology that others have dismissed or pushing for a radical product redesign that defies conventional wisdom. It's about understanding that while the present is important, the future is where true success lies.

For modern executives, this also means knowing when to disrupt the status quo in your organization. Change can be uncomfortable, but if you can see a future that others don't, your job as a leader is to guide them through it.

Visionary Leadership in Today's Business World

In today's fast-paced, technology-driven business world, the importance of visionary leadership cannot be overstated. Just as Rome's greatest leaders reshaped their empire, modern entrepreneurs and executives must reshape their industries and organizations. The speed of innovation means that companies can either evolve or be left behind. (Rome waited for no one!)

A modern example of visionary leadership is Elon Musk, whose ability to see beyond the present has propelled companies including SpaceX, Tesla, Neuralink, xAI, and the Boring Company to the forefront of their industries. Musk saw electric vehicles and space exploration as more than simply business niches; he saw them as the future. He recognized that the world's reliance on fossil fuels was unsustainable, and instead of waiting for the market to catch up, he led the charge. This ability to see beyond the horizon is what separates truly transformational leaders from those who simply follow trends.

Case Study II: Augustus and the Power of Long-Term Thinking

While Julius Caesar laid the groundwork, it was his successor Augustus who truly transformed Rome into the global power it would become. Augustus was the kind of leader who sought more than short-term wins. Instead, he played the long game. After decades of civil war and instability, Augustus's aim was to stabilize Rome. Ultimately, he wanted to build a foundation for long-term peace and prosperity.

His reign marked the beginning of the *Pax Romana*, a period of relative peace that lasted for over two centuries. Augustus achieved this by implementing reforms that would ensure Rome's success well into the future. He reorganized the military, rebuilt the city of Rome, and established a system of taxation that allowed for sustained economic growth.

Empire of Influence Takeaway:

For modern executives, the lesson from Augustus is clear: successful leadership requires a balance between managing the present crises and building for the future. Augustus responded to the chaos of his time while positioning to meet the anticipated needs of future generations. In today's business environment, executives must focus not just on quarterly earnings but on sustainable, long-term growth.

This could mean investing in talent development, building robust infrastructure, or fostering innovation. A visionary leader understands that decisions made today have ripple effects that will shape the future of the organization.

Startups and entrepreneurs can also learn from Augustus' long-term approach. While early-stage companies often focus on rapid growth and scalability, they should also think beyond immediate gains. This is essential. What kind of company do you want to build ten or twenty years from now? What values and systems are you putting in place today that will support that vision?

The Visionary Mindset: Shifting from Reactive to Proactive Leadership

One of the key qualities that separates visionary leaders from the rest is their ability to shift from reactive to proactive leadership. In the Roman Empire, leaders who merely reacted to crises often found themselves overwhelmed by the sheer complexity of their challenges. Those who succeeded, for instance, Julius Caesar and Caesar Augustus (Octavian), were able to look ahead, anticipate problems, and take preemptive action.

In the modern business world, Jeff Bezos exemplifies this shift. As the founder of Amazon, he anticipated the changes in the retail industry and moved to position for success. In the early 2000s, Bezos recognized that the future of commerce was digital and made bold investments in technology, logistics, and cloud computing. While other retailers were struggling to catch up with e-commerce, Bezos was already planning for the next phase of

Amazon's growth. His focus was on leading the digital revolution, not merely being a participant.

Case Study III: Florence Nightingale and the Power of Vision in Healthcare

Let's step out of ancient Rome for a moment and look at one of the most influential healthcare leaders in history: Florence Nightingale. Known as the founder of modern nursing, Nightingale's contributions to healthcare were revolutionary, not just because of what she did, but because of what she envisioned.

In the mid-1800s, healthcare was often chaotic and unorganized. During the Crimean War, hospitals were overcrowded, unsanitary, and ill-equipped to care for the injured. Florence Nightingale recognized this and set about creating a system that would not only improve care in the immediate moment but also provide a lasting framework for the future of healthcare. She introduced sanitation practices, established nursing standards, and restructured hospital management, significantly reducing mortality rates.

Nightingale's visionary approach to healthcare reform not only improved the conditions during the war; her impact reshaped the entire healthcare system for generations to come. She understood that *lasting change requires both immediate action and long-term thinking,* a lesson that today's healthcare executives can take to heart.

Visionary Leadership in Healthcare: The Case for Telemedicine

Today's healthcare leaders must also balance the immediate needs of their patients with a vision for the future. One example of this is the rise of telemedicine. Before the COVID-19 pandemic, telemedicine was often viewed as a secondary option for patient care, with many healthcare systems slow to adopt it. But the pandemic forced healthcare leaders to rethink the way care was delivered, and telemedicine emerged as a critical tool for ensuring patient access.

Visionary healthcare leaders not only adapted to the crisis but also saw telemedicine as a long-term solution beyond the pandemic. They recognized that telemedicine could improve access to care, reduce costs, and increase efficiency in the healthcare system. These leaders were able to see beyond the immediate need and envision a future where digital health plays a central role in patient care.

Special Section for Healthcare Executives: Visionary Leadership

For healthcare executives, visionary leadership is a necessity. There is no other alternative. The healthcare industry is undergoing rapid transformation, driven by technological advances, policy changes, and shifting patient expectations. Leaders who can anticipate these changes and act proactively will be the ones who shape the future of healthcare.

Anticipating Technological Change: Visionary healthcare leaders must stay ahead of the curve when it comes to technology. Whether it's artificial intelligence (AI), telemedicine, or wearable health devices, the future of healthcare is increasingly digital. Healthcare executives must embrace these technologies and prioritize integrating them into their long-term strategies for improving patient outcomes, reducing costs, and streamlining operations.

Building Sustainable Healthcare Models: Visionary healthcare executives understand that sustainability is key to long-term success. This requires not only focusing on short-term gains, but also continually building systems that can withstand future challenges. This is essential, whether it's a public health crisis, changes in policy, or shifts in patient demographics. Sustainability in healthcare is about creating models that are both adaptable and resilient.

Leading through Crisis: Just as Florence Nightingale saw beyond the immediate chaos of the Crimean War to create a lasting framework for modern healthcare, today's healthcare leaders must use crises as opportunities for innovation. The COVID-19 pandemic has shown that healthcare systems need to be flexible and versatile. Visionary leaders are those who can take the lessons learned from a crisis and apply them to future challenges.

Fostering a Culture of Innovation: Visionary healthcare executives constantly read, explore, listen, and foster a culture of innovation and create the time and space to make it a reality. This means establishing an environment where healthcare providers are empowered to suggest new ideas, experiment with new technologies, and challenge the status quo. It also means investing in leadership development to ensure that the next generation of healthcare leaders is equipped to handle the challenges of tomorrow.

Reflection Questions

1. *Vision and Risk-Taking:*
   Think about a time when you had to take a significant risk to pursue your vision. What did you learn from that experience, and how did it shape your approach to leadership?

How can you apply visionary risk-taking in your current role? What bold decisions can you make today to shape the future of your business or healthcare organization?

2. *Long-Term Planning:*
    Are you focusing too much on short-term results at the expense of long-term growth? How can you better balance immediate needs with long-term planning in your organization?

    What systems, processes, or strategies can you put in place now that will ensure your organization's success ten, twenty, or even fifty years from now?

3. *Innovation and Crisis Management:*
    How have you handled crises in the past? Were you able to use those moments as opportunities to innovate and reshape your organization?

    What are some emerging trends or technologies in your industry that you can proactively adopt to stay ahead of the curve?

4. *Visionary Leadership in Healthcare:*
    As a healthcare executive, how are you integrating new technologies like AI, telemedicine, or wearable health devices into your organization's long-term strategy?

    What steps are you taking to ensure that your healthcare system is sustainable and resilient in the face of future challenges?

Final Thoughts: Visionary Leadership for a Changing World

In both ancient Rome and modern times, visionary leaders are those who can look beyond the challenges of the present and move to shape the future. Whether you're leading a healthcare organization, running a startup, or managing a large corporation, your ability to anticipate changes, take bold risks, and think long-term will define your success. Visionary leadership is not merely anticipating the future, but creating it.

Obiter Dictum:

Visionary leadership is about preparing for the future with clarity, discipline, and commitment. In both ancient and modern leadership, a great power lies in anticipation. I have seen firsthand in healthcare and business alike: the leaders who thrive are those who balance immediate pressures with bold, future-focused thinking. It is not about guessing or ego. Whether you are building clinical systems or scaling a new venture, remember that long-term, sustainable success is rooted in purposeful planning and the courage to lead through uncertainty. Build with the future in mind, your legacy depends on it.

Scenario:

A tempting shortcut promises immediate profits but risks long-term brand trust.

What Would a Worthy Roman Imperator Do?

Emulate Augustus: Think centuries, not quarters. Build enduring structures, even if patience strains ambition. True vision always outlasts short-lived applause.

Vision sets the course, but boldness breaks the barriers. Once the groundwork of foresight is laid, the true conundrum is disrupting norms to bring that vision into reality. Let us now meet the rebels who changed the rules, and the world.

"Fortune favors the bold."

–Virgil

CHAPTER III

Rebels with a Cause: Disrupting Like a Roman General

Focus: Innovation often means challenging convention. This chapter highlights the courage required to break molds, defy norms, and reshape systems.

In a world that moves at lightning speed, innovation and disruption are no longer optional, they are essential. Today's most successful entrepreneurs and executives are not the ones who simply maintain the status quo. They are the ones who break through boundaries, question norms, and turn industries upside down to create something entirely new. This chapter dives into the lives and leadership styles of innovators and disruptors throughout history, particularly in ancient Rome, and connects their boldness to modern business and healthcare landscapes.

By reading this chapter, you'll discover how today's leaders can embrace disruptive thinking, navigate resistance, and drive significant change in their industries. You'll also learn practical strategies for fostering innovation in your organization, positioning yourself and your team for long-term success.

The Disruptor's Mindset: Breaking Traditions and Challenging Norms

In any field, there comes a time when doing things the way they have always been done is simply not good enough. Ancient Rome had its share of disruptors, people who broke away from traditions and sparked revolutions in politics, science, and medicine. These disruptors were not reckless; they had a vision that extended beyond the immediate horizon.

Emperor Claudius

Claudius (41–54 AD) might be the most surprising emperor in Roman history. Written off as weak and ineffectual due to his physical disabilities, he was often mocked by his own family. But when the Praetorian Guard unexpectedly declared him emperor after Caligula's assassination, Claudius proved everyone wrong. Not only did he survive in a role few expected him to excel in, he thrived. In fact, he became one of Rome's most innovative and reformist leaders.

From Outcast to Emperor

Claudius didn't fit the Roman image of a leader. He stammered, walked with a limp, and was sidelined by his family for most of his life. Yet his time in the shadows gave him a keen intellect and a deep understanding of Roman politics, history, and administration. When he became emperor, he approached the role with the precision of a scholar and the determination of an underdog.

One of his boldest moves was the conquest of Britain, a feat that had eluded even Julius Caesar. Claudius invaded Britain and established Roman rule with infrastructure, roads, and governance. He ensured the conquest was sustainable.

An Administrative Reformer

Claudius was also a disruptor in Roman bureaucracy. He appointed "Freedmen" (former slaves) to key government positions, breaking the traditional mold of relying solely on aristocrats. While this earned him criticism from Rome's elite, it brought fresh talent into the administration and improved efficiency.

He also reformed the legal system, taking an active role in hearing cases and ensuring justice. Even if it meant challenging tradition, Claudius ultimately believed that leadership was about improvement and influential action.

Lessons for Modern Leaders

Your setbacks can be your strength. Claudius's time as an outcast gave him unique insights and resilience. Leaders today can use their own challenges as opportunities to grow and think differently.

Look beyond traditional talent pools. Claudius's appointment of freedmen to government positions shows the value of breaking hierarchies and bringing in diverse perspectives. Modern leaders should focus on potential and skill rather than pedigree.

Bold moves lead to big results. Claudius's conquest of Britain was not only a military triumph; it was a legacy-builder. Leaders who take calculated risks can achieve extraordinary results.

Breaking the Mold

Claudius' story is a reminder that leadership doesn't necessarily fit a predetermined mold, in fact, it can be about reshaping it. His ability to rise above doubt and deliver meaningful reforms makes him a timeless example of innovation under pressure.

Let's examine one Roman general and how he invigorated the military: Gaius Marius. He was a Roman general and statesman who radically reformed the Roman military. Before his time, only wealthy landowners were allowed to serve as soldiers. But Marius, seeing an opportunity to strengthen Rome's forces, broke with tradition and opened military service to the common people. This was a seismic shift in Roman society. The reform not only strengthened the army but also changed the social fabric of Rome by giving the lower classes new opportunities for upward mobility.

Today's entrepreneurs and executives face a similar challenge: to recognize when the old ways of doing things no longer serve their purpose and to push for change. This may mean *upending traditional business models*, embracing new technologies, or fostering a culture of innovation in industries that are typically resistant to change.

Case Study I: Netflix—Breaking the Rules of Entertainment

In the early 2000s, Netflix was a DVD rental service trying to compete with Blockbuster, which at the time dominated the market. But instead of just fighting for market share, Netflix disrupted the entire industry by moving to a subscription-based streaming model, a move that was bold and risky. Founder Reed Hastings understood that the future of entertainment wasn't in physical rentals, but in digital streaming.

The switch didn't happen overnight, and Netflix faced resistance—not just from competitors but from consumers who were used to renting DVDs. However, Hastings and his team pushed forward, betting on a future where content would be instantly accessible online. Today, Netflix's streaming model is the industry standard, and the company has transformed how the world consumes entertainment.

Like Gaius Marius opening the legions to the lower classes, Netflix democratized access to entertainment.

Empire of Influence Takeaway:

Disruption does not mean destruction; it means reinvention. Reed Hastings did not destroy the entertainment industry. He reinvented it by leveraging technology and access, ultimately changing consumer behavior.

As an entrepreneur or executive, don't be afraid to *break the mold* of your industry. Often, playing by the old rules limits your potential. Look for ways to innovate and disrupt, even if it means facing initial resistance.

The Courage to Be Different: Marie Curie and Disruptive Innovation in Science

While Gaius Marius revolutionized the military, innovators in other fields were also reshaping their worlds. One of the most inspiring examples of disruptive innovation in science is Marie Curie. She was an extraordinary scientist who shattered societal norms and scientific conventions. Marie Curie was a true trailblazer.

In the early 20th century, Curie made groundbreaking discoveries in radioactivity, a field that was completely uncharted at the time. But her path wasn't easy. As a woman in a male-dominated field, she faced immense challenges, from institutional bias to limited access to research resources. Yet, despite these obstacles, Curie's work transformed our understanding of physics and chemistry. She was not content to merely advance within the existing scientific community; she disrupted the paradigms and pioneered a whole new field of study.

Empire of Influence Takeaway:

Disruptive innovation often requires you to *challenge the prevailing norms*, even if that means going against the grain. In Curie's case, this meant conducting experiments that other scientists didn't think were possible.

As a leader, *are you fostering a culture where innovation can flourish*, or are you inadvertently reinforcing the status quo? The ability to embrace new ideas, even when they challenge long-held beliefs, is crucial to leading disruptive change.

Case Study II: Tesla—Leading Disruption in the Auto Industry

In the 21st century, few industries have been as ripe for disruption as the automotive industry. For over a century, cars were powered by internal combustion engines, and innovation in the sector seemed to plateau. Enter Elon Musk and Tesla.

When Musk set out to build an electric car, his vision sought to reinvent how the world thinks about transportation. At the time Tesla launched, electric vehicles were considered impractical and niche. But Musk didn't let industry norms stop him. He challenged the conventional wisdom that electric cars couldn't compete with gas-powered vehicles in performance, design, or appeal. Through relentless innovation and a clear vision, Musk turned Tesla into one of the most valuable automakers in the world, pushing the entire industry toward an innovative and greener future.

Empire of Influence Takeaway:

Visionary leaders are not passive devotees of industry norms; they are challengers. Tesla redefined what an automobile could be, and Musk's team created a product that pushed both technological and cultural boundaries.

In your business, what are the entrenched beliefs that might be limiting your potential? How can you create a disruptive force that challenges these assumptions and offers a new way of thinking?

Navigating Resistance: Overcoming Barriers to Disruption

It's easy to talk about disruption, but the reality is that innovation often meets resistance. In ancient Rome, disruptors like Julius Caesar faced immense pushback from the Senate and the established elites. The same is true for today's innovators.

One reason for this resistance is that disruption creates *uncertainty*. People and organizations are often hesitant to embrace change, particularly when that change threatens their existing way of doing things. However, as a leader, it is your responsibility to navigate this resistance and keep pushing forward. *Disruption is the impetus to overcome resistance, not avoid it.*

Let's look at Henry Ford for a moment. When Ford introduced the Model T, he was selling a car and changing the world by promoting a new way of life for the multitude. At the time, cars were a luxury item, and most people relied on horses for transportation. Ford faced significant skepticism, both from competitors and potential customers. Yet, he believed in the power of mass production through specialization to streamline the process; the result was low-cost automobiles for greater public consumption. His ability to make cars affordable for the average consumer transformed transportation and, in doing so, created one of the most influential industries in modern history.

Case Study III: Uber—Disrupting the Transportation Industry

One of the most disruptive innovations in recent history is Uber.

Before Uber, the taxi industry operated with a tried-and-true model: licensed drivers, centralized dispatch systems, and fixed fares. The idea that anyone with a car and a smartphone could become a driver, and that consumers could hail a ride through an app, was a radical proposal.

Founders Travis Kalanick and Garrett Camp faced significant legal and regulatory hurdles as they attempted to disrupt the taxi industry. Established taxi companies, municipalities, and even drivers pushed back hard against Uber's model. However, Kalanick and Camp persisted. They recognized that the demand for convenience and lower prices would ultimately win out. Uber's success forced the entire transportation industry to rethink its business model. Ride-sharing services have since become the global norm.

Empire of Influence Takeaway:

Disrupting an industry often means navigating resistance from incumbents. Whether that resistance comes from regulators, competitors, or even consumers themselves, leaders must be prepared to face opposition.

Resilience is key. Kalanick and Camp refused to back down when facing regulatory challenges; they fought for their vision. As a leader, are you ready to push through obstacles to bring your disruptive ideas to life?

The Power of Small Disruptions: Joseph Lister and Medical Innovation

Not every disruption needs to be massive. Sometimes, small innovations can have an outsized impact. One such innovator was Joseph Lister, a 19th-century British surgeon who revolutionized medicine by introducing antiseptic surgery. At the time, infections following surgeries were rampant, and many believed that infections were an inevitable outcome of surgery. Lister, however, thought differently. He hypothesized that microorganisms were responsible for infections and began using carbolic acid to sterilize surgical instruments and clean wounds.

The idea of sterilization wasn't initially embraced by the medical community, and Lister faced skepticism and resistance from his peers. Yet his antiseptic methods proved to be effective, drastically reducing postoperative infections and deaths. Lister's innovation, though seemingly simple, fundamentally transformed surgical practices and saved countless lives.

Empire of Influence Takeaway:

Small changes can lead to significant disruptions. Lister didn't reinvent the entire field of surgery; he introduced a small, practical innovation that reshaped medical practices.

As a leader, don't overlook the power of *incremental innovations*. Sometimes, the smallest disruptions can have the most profound impact on your organization and industry.

Special Section for Healthcare Executives: Disruptive Innovation

Disruption is not only happening in the business world, it is also occurring at an extreme pace in healthcare. In fact, the healthcare industry is one of the sectors most in need of disruptive thinking and action. With rising costs, inefficiencies, and an increasingly complex regulatory environment, healthcare leaders must continue to *challenge the traditional ways of delivering care.*

Embracing Telemedicine: The COVID-19 pandemic rapidly accelerated the adoption of telemedicine, but this disruption has been a long time coming. Forward-thinking healthcare executives recognize that telemedicine cannot be only a stopgap solution, instead, it must continually progress as a powerful tool for increasing access to care, improving efficiency, and reducing costs. The next challenge for healthcare leaders is to fully integrate telemedicine into their systems, making it a permanent fixture of patient care.

> *Leadership Tip:* Embrace technology as a way to disrupt traditional healthcare delivery models. Are there new ways to provide care that challenge the norms but benefit both patients and providers?

AI and Machine Learning: Artificial intelligence (AI) and machine learning are poised to disrupt the healthcare industry in profound ways. From diagnostic tools to personalized treatment plans, AI is already being used to improve patient outcomes and streamline healthcare processes. However, the full potential of AI in healthcare has yet to be realized.

> *Leadership Tip:* Start thinking about how AI can disrupt your healthcare organization. How can you use data to predict patient needs, improve the caregivers' environment, enhance diagnoses, streamline the revenue cycle, and reduce operational inefficiencies?

Patient-Centered Care Models: For decades, healthcare has been provider-centric, with doctors, nurses, and administrators driving care decisions. But in recent years, a shift has begun toward patient-centered care, where patients are more empowered to make decisions about their health. Disruptive healthcare leaders are embracing this model, putting patients at the center of the care continuum and leveraging digital tools to give patients more control over their health.

Leadership Tip: Keep asking yourself: how can your healthcare organization continue its shift toward a more patient-centered model? What technologies, processes, and innovations can you implement to make care more accessible, personalized, and patient-friendly?

Reflection Questions

1. *Embracing Disruption:*

   Think about an area of your industry that is ripe for disruption. What entrenched beliefs or practices are holding back innovation, and how can you challenge them?

   Are there small, incremental innovations you can implement in your organization that could have a big impact?

2. *Overcoming Resistance:*

   Reflect on a time when you faced resistance to a new idea or innovation. How did you handle it, and what could you have done differently to overcome the obstacles?

   In your current role, what resistance might you face when attempting to introduce disruptive innovations, and how can you prepare to navigate that resistance?

3. *Fostering Innovation:*

   As a leader, are you creating a culture that encourages innovation, or are you reinforcing the status quo? What can you do to foster a more disruptive and innovative mindset within your team?

How can you ensure that your organization is constantly evolving and adapting to new trends and technologies?

4. *Disruptive Innovation in Healthcare:*
    How can your healthcare organization embrace telemedicine, AI, or patient-centered care at a higher level to disrupt traditional healthcare delivery models?

    What regulatory or operational hurdles might you face when implementing disruptive innovations in healthcare, and how can you address them proactively?

Final Thoughts: Leading the Charge of Innovation and Disruption

Innovators and disruptors are profound thinkers and doers. They see the cracks in the existing system and have the courage to create something new. Whether you're in healthcare or running a startup, the ability to *challenge the status quo and lead disruptive change* is essential for long-term success. As you reflect on the lessons from this chapter, consider how you can push the boundaries of your industry and create lasting impact through innovation.

Obiter Dictum:

Disruption is about courage, not merely technology or innovation. Throughout my career in healthcare, I have seen the tension between protecting legacy systems and pushing for necessary transformation. Leaders who stand out are the ones willing to challenge assumptions. It is not for the sake of rebellion, but to create meaningful, measurable improvement. As you lead in your own organization, ask yourself: where are we defaulting to day-to-day comfort over meaningful change driven courage? True progress often requires breaking the mold; moreover, it is always with integrity, purpose, and the necessary discipline and focus determining each step.

Scenario:

You spot a disruptive innovation but face ridicule from industry "experts."

What Would a Worthy Roman Imperator Do?

Be like Gaius Marius. Break the mold. Recruit new talent, revise broken systems, and innovate where others cling to tradition. Progress demands rebellion.

Disruption demands courage, but sustaining transformation requires a moral compass. With innovation pushing boundaries, we must ask: who ensures the lines of integrity are not blurred? The answer lies in principled leadership.

*"The wise are instructed by reason, average minds
by experience, the stupid by necessity and the brute
by instinct. Integrity of men is to be measured
by their conduct, not by their professions."*

–Cicero

CHAPTER IV

The Moral Standard: Integrity from Forum to Boardroom

*Focus: Ethical leadership builds trust, resilience,
and legacy. In Rome and today, moral courage
separates the powerful from the principled.*

L eadership often requires an intense focus on innovation, disruption, or driving profits. However, at its core, effective leadership is about making decisions that are grounded in *ethics and integrity*. While it's tempting to prioritize short-term gains, the most successful leaders know that their legacy is built on a foundation of ethical choices that inspire trust, loyalty, and respect. This chapter explores how ethics shape leadership in healthcare, business, and beyond, using examples from ancient Rome and modern case studies to show how leaders today can navigate complex ethical dilemmas with integrity.

We'll uncover how ethical leadership is not simply a preferred trait, but the key characteristic that holds high-functioning teams and organizations together. Whether you're an entrepreneur building a startup or a healthcare executive steering a massive health system, this chapter will provide valuable insights into making decisions that stand the test of time.

Antoninus Pius

Antoninus Pius (138–161 AD) is often overshadowed by his predecessor Hadrian and his successor Marcus Aurelius, but his reign is a quiet masterpiece of ethical and steady leadership. His nickname, "Pius," reflects his devotion to duty, fairness, and morality. His reign was one of the most peaceful and prosperous in Roman history.

The Peaceful Administrator

Unlike other emperors, Antoninus avoided military conquests, focusing instead on internal reforms and governance. He introduced significant legal reforms, particularly to protect the rights of slaves and improve the fairness of trials. He believed that justice required a process of punishing the guilty but also instituting safeguards to protect the vulnerable.

Antoninus also invested in public infrastructure, funding aqueducts, roads, and temples. His philosophy was simple: leadership is about service, not power.

Lessons for Modern Leaders

Lead with fairness. Antoninus's legal reforms remind us that ethical leadership builds trust and stability. Leaders today can emulate this by fostering fairness and transparency in decision-making.

Avoid unnecessary conflict. Antoninus' peaceful reign shows the power of focusing on internal growth rather than external battles. Modern leaders can prioritize building strong foundations over chasing endless expansion.

Serve your people. Like Antoninus' investments in infrastructure, leaders can create lasting impact by prioritizing the well-being of their teams and communities.

Legacy of a Quiet Leader

Antoninus's reign might not have been filled with drama, but it proved that leadership does not have to be loud to be effective. His steady hand and moral compass left Rome stronger than he found it, a testament to the enduring power of ethical governance.

Ethical Leadership in Ancient Rome: The Power of Honor and Duty

Ancient Rome was an empire built on military might, with its foundation rooted in a society where honor, duty, and ethics played a critical role in leadership. This was instrumental in leading to its long-term success. Romans believed that a leader's actions reflected their moral character, and this was particularly evident in the figure of Cincinnatus.

Cincinnatus, a Roman statesman and general, is famous for his humility and integrity.

It's impossible to talk about leadership without addressing ethics and integrity. In healthcare, these are often central concerns. But they should also be at the heart of business leadership.

In 458 BC, Rome was under attack, and Cincinnatus was appointed as a temporary dictator to lead the defense. Cincinnatus was a farmer called to serve during a time of crisis. After successfully defeating Rome's enemies, he did something almost unheard of: he relinquished his absolute power and returned to his farm. In a society where power was often hoarded, Cincinnatus became a symbol of selflessness, placing the needs of the republic above personal ambition. His humility, integrity, and sense of duty made him one of Rome's most revered figures. Roman leaders like Cincinnatus became legendary not for their conquests but for their moral fortitude.

What's the lesson here? Leadership is about knowing when to serve, how to serve, and when to step aside to pass the power to another. In today's world, where scandals often plague corporations and ethical breaches can bring entire organizations to their knees, Cincinnatus reminds us that integrity and service should always come first.

In healthcare and business alike, ethical leadership builds trust. Your patients, employees, and customers are more likely to trust and remain loyal to you if they believe that you are operating with transparency and moral integrity.

Cicero was a tireless advocate for moral responsibility, and his work, particularly his treatise *De Officiis* (On Duties)**,** emphasizes that a leader's foremost duty is to uphold justice, fairness, and the common good. This can offer a strong foundation for discussing how modern leaders must balance personal ambition with public responsibility.

Cicero and the Foundation of Ethical Leadership

Why Cicero? In his life and writings, Cicero championed the idea that *leadership must be rooted in ethics* and that personal ambition should always be subordinate to the public good. In *De Officiis*, he outlines the duties of leaders and how they must act with integrity, balancing self-interest with the welfare of society. Cicero's thoughts can be particularly instructive for modern executives who are often pulled between short-term gains and long-term ethical responsibilities.

Cicero faced numerous ethical dilemmas, including being exiled for standing up to powerful political forces. Yet, his unwavering belief in justice and his refusal to compromise on his moral principles solidified his legacy. His leadership and ethical philosophy have endured for centuries, and his life provides a compelling narrative of standing firm in one's values, even when the consequences are dire.

Key Leadership Lesson from Cicero: Leaders must be guided by a moral compass that points to the greater good. Success that comes at the expense of ethical integrity is hollow and unsustainable. Cicero believed that the true legacy of a leader is built not only through power and wealth but through adherence to *virtue, justice, and duty.*

Case Study Application: Cicero's philosophy mirrors the ethical decision-making process demonstrated by companies like Merck & Co., which chose to prioritize human lives over profits when it provided Mectizan for free to combat river blindness. This act of corporate responsibility echoes Cicero's insistence that the highest duty of a leader is to serve the common good.

Empire of Influence Takeaway:

Leaders should reflect on how their decisions affect the broader community. Are they prioritizing the public good over personal or organizational gain? Cicero's life teaches us that true leadership lies in serving the common good, even when the personal cost is high.

Are you willing to make decisions that uphold ethical integrity, even when it means facing opposition or personal sacrifice?

Nero (as a counterexample)

Ah, Nero. The name itself conjures images of fiddling while Rome burned, a story that may not be entirely true but captures the essence of his self-serving leadership. Nero (37–68 AD) is infamous for his extravagance, paranoia, and mismanagement, making him the perfect cautionary tale for modern leaders.

Lavish Excess

Nero's reign began with promise. He reduced taxes, promoted cultural events, and even performed as an artist. But as time went on, his priorities shifted. He built the "Domus Aurea" (Golden House), a massive palace that sprawled across Rome, displacing entire neighborhoods. The palace was a symbol of Nero's focus on personal pleasure rather than public welfare.

The Great Fire of Rome

In 64 AD, a massive fire devastated Rome. While there's no evidence that Nero actually "fiddled" during the blaze (violins hadn't been invented yet), his response was disastrous. Instead of addressing the needs of the people, Nero used the opportunity to expand his palace. The public blamed him for the fire, and his popularity plummeted.

Leadership Lesson

Nero's reign is a reminder of what happens when leaders prioritize personal ambition over organizational health. Transparency, accountability, and empathy are essential to maintaining trust and stability.

The Legacy of Failure

Nero's story ended in rebellion and suicide, leaving behind

a tarnished legacy. For modern leaders, Nero's failures serve as a reminder that ethical leadership and public trust are the cornerstones of success.

Case Study I: The Fall of Enron—A Cautionary Tale of Ethical Collapse

No chapter on ethics would be complete without discussing *Enron*, the energy company that became synonymous with corporate fraud and scandal in the early 2000s. Once lauded as a highly innovative company, two of Enron's leaders, CEO Jeffrey Skilling and Chairman Kenneth Lay, were involved in one of the most notorious corporate fraud schemes in history.

The company's collapse was driven by unethical financial practices, including hiding billions of dollars in debt through off-the-books partnerships. What's more, Enron encouraged a culture of reckless ambition, in which executives prioritized personal gains over ethical considerations. When the fraud was exposed, Enron went bankrupt, employees lost their jobs and pensions, and its top leaders were imprisoned.

Empire of Influence Takeaway:

Ethics cannot be an afterthought in business. The fall of Enron demonstrates how ethical shortcuts can lead to massive, long-term consequences for both leaders and the organizations they run.

As an entrepreneur or executive, you must build a culture of transparency and accountability. Even in high-pressure situations, your decisions should prioritize *ethical responsibility* over short-term profits.

Enron's story is a reminder that without a strong ethical compass, even the most successful companies can collapse under the weight of their own dishonesty.

Building an Ethical Culture: Leading by Example

Creating a culture of ethics and integrity starts at the top. Leaders set the tone for the entire organization. If leaders cut corners, their teams will, too. But when leaders prioritize ethics, they inspire the same level of integrity throughout the company.

Let's take a moment to consider Patagonia, the outdoor clothing company known for its environmental activism. Founder Yvon Chouinard built Patagonia on a foundation of environmental and ethical responsibility. The company donates 1% of its profits to environmental causes and encourages customers to repair their gear rather than buy new items. Chouinard's ethical stance has earned Patagonia not only a loyal customer base but also immense respect in the business community.

Patagonia's leadership is an example of how *aligning business goals with ethical values* can drive long-term success. Customers and employees are drawn to companies that stand for something beyond profit, and when leaders stay true to their ethical principles, they build a foundation of trust that can weather any storm.

Empire of Influence Takeaway:

Ethical leadership starts with *transparency, honesty, and consistency*. As a leader, your actions should align with your stated values; every decision you make should reinforce the ethical culture you want to build.

Companies that put ethics at the center of their decision-making are more likely to inspire loyalty from customers and employees, leading to long-term success.

Case Study II: Johnson & Johnson—Managing the Tylenol Crisis with Integrity

One of the best examples of ethical leadership in the face of crisis comes from Johnson & Johnson. In 1982, the company faced a major crisis when several people died after taking Tylenol that had been laced with cyanide. Although the fact that the contamination occurred outside of the company's control, Johnson & Johnson took immediate and decisive action. The company issued a nationwide recall of 31 million bottles of Tylenol, costing over $100 million, and introduced tamper-proof packaging that would later become the industry standard.

Johnson & Johnson's swift and ethical response to the crisis earned the company widespread praise and restored consumer confidence. The company's actions were guided by its corporate credo, which emphasized responsibility to customers, employees, and the community.

Empire of Influence Takeaway:

Ethical leadership is tested in moments of crisis. Johnson & Johnson's response to the Tylenol crisis demonstrates that when leaders prioritize ethics over profits, they not only protect their brand but also build trust with consumers.

As a leader, it is essential to have a clear *moral framework* in place before a crisis hits. Decisions made under pressure should still align with your core values and ethical commitments. It is imperative that this clarity focuses you on the next step, regardless of all the immediate and urgent distractions.

The Long-Term Value of Ethical Leadership

One of the most important aspects of ethical leadership is the long-term perspective it brings. Leaders who prioritize ethics may not always see immediate rewards, but over time, they build a legacy that is far more valuable than short-term gains. Ethical leaders are remembered not just for their success but for the positive impact they leave on their organizations and the people they serve.

In ancient Rome, this long-term perspective can again be seen in the leadership of Marcus Aurelius, the Stoic philosopher-emperor. Despite holding ultimate power, Marcus Aurelius governed with humility, integrity, and a commitment to the well-being of his people. His writings in *Meditations* reveal a leader who was constantly striving to act in accordance with his ethical beliefs, even in the face of war, plague, and political strife.

Marcus Aurelius's leadership is a reminder that ethical decision-making is more than just following the rules or obeying the Compliance department. In fact, to emulate his example is to lead with *compassion, fairness, and a deep sense of responsibility.* It is the ideal for the people you serve.

Empire of Influence Takeaway:

Ethical leadership requires a long-term view. *Short-term sacrifices for ethical integrity* often result in long-term trust and loyalty from both employees and customers.

The most respected leaders are not those who amass the most power or wealth, but those who build organizations that are rooted in integrity and compassion.

Case Study III: Starbucks—A Commitment to Ethical Sourcing

Another modern example of long-term ethical leadership is Starbucks. The global coffee giant has built its brand not only on its products but also on its commitment to ethical sourcing. Starbucks was one of the first companies to develop comprehensive guidelines for buying ethically grown and traded coffee, partnering with farmers around the world to ensure sustainable practices.

This commitment to ethics has paid off. Starbucks customers are willing to pay a premium for coffee because they trust that the company is doing the right thing. Starbucks's ethical leadership has become a core part of its brand identity, attracting customers who value sustainability and fairness.

Empire of Influence Takeaway:

Ethical leadership is more than just an application to utilize during crisis management; it should be woven into the very fabric of your business model. Starbucks' success shows that customers appreciate companies that prioritize ethical practices in every aspect of their operations.

Long-term success is built on trust. By ensuring that your business practices align with your ethical values, you can build a brand that stands the test of time.

Ethical Leadership in Healthcare: Navigating Complex Moral Dilemmas

In healthcare, ethical leadership is particularly critical because decisions often involve life and death, patient privacy, and access to care. Healthcare leaders must not only manage their organizations but also navigate complex moral dilemmas that directly affect patient outcomes.

Case Study IV: Dr. Frances Oldham Kelsey— A Stand for Ethics in Drug Approval

In the early 1960s, Dr. Frances Oldham Kelsey was a medical officer at the U.S. Food and Drug Administration (FDA). During her time at the FDA, Kelsey reviewed the application for thalidomide, a drug that was already being widely used in Europe to treat nausea in pregnant women. Despite pressure from the drug's manufacturer to approve it quickly, Kelsey refused, citing a lack of sufficient safety data.

Her decision was vindicated when it was later discovered that thalidomide caused severe birth defects. Kelsey's ethical stand prevented the drug from being approved in the U.S. and saved countless lives. Her commitment to patient safety, even in the face of industry pressure, is a powerful example of ethical leadership in healthcare.

Healthcare Executive Takeaway:

Ethical leadership in healthcare often requires *resisting external pressures* and making decisions that prioritize patient safety and well-being.

As a healthcare leader, you must create an organizational culture that prioritizes ethical decision-making and patient care over financial or operational convenience.

Special Section for Healthcare Executives: Ethical Leadership

Healthcare executives face unique ethical challenges that often involve difficult trade-offs between cost, access, and quality of care. Unlike other industries, healthcare decisions directly impact human lives, which means that the stakes are incredibly high. Ethical leadership is not optional; it is essential to maintaining trust with patients, employees, and the public.

Balancing Cost and Care: Healthcare executives are often tasked with making decisions that balance the financial viability of their organization with the need to provide high-quality care.

This can create ethical dilemmas, such as deciding how to allocate limited resources or how to handle patients who cannot afford treatment.

Leadership Tip: Develop clear ethical guidelines that prioritize patient care while maintaining financial responsibility. Ensure transparency in decision-making processes, ensuring that all stakeholders understand the ethical considerations behind resource allocation.

Patient Privacy and Data Ethics: With the increasing use of digital health tools and electronic medical records, healthcare executives must navigate the ethical challenges of patient privacy and data security. Ensuring that patient data is protected and used ethically is critical for maintaining trust.

Leadership Tip: Invest in cybersecurity and data governance protocols that prioritize patient privacy. Ensure that your organization complies with regulations like HIPAA while also educating your staff on the importance of ethical data use.

Equitable Access to Care: One of the most pressing ethical issues in healthcare is ensuring equitable access to care. Healthcare executives must work to eliminate disparities in healthcare access based on race, socioeconomic status, and geography.

Leadership Tip: Advocate for policies and initiatives that promote equitable care. This could include expanding telemedicine services to underserved areas or partnering with community organizations to improve healthcare access for vulnerable populations.

Fostering an Ethical Organizational Culture: Ethical leadership is about making the right decisions at every level. It is about creating an organizational culture that promotes ethics at all levels. Healthcare executives must lead by example, setting high ethical standards and ensuring that those standards are maintained throughout the organization.

> *Leadership Tip:* Regularly train your staff on ethical decision-making and establish clear channels for reporting unethical behavior. Ensure that ethics are embedded in every part of your organization, from patient care to administrative practices.

Reflection Questions

1. *Navigating Ethical Dilemmas:*
   Reflect on a time when you faced an ethical dilemma in your leadership role. How did you handle it, and what factors influenced your decision-making process? In hindsight, is there anything you would have done differently?

   What ethical dilemmas do you anticipate in your current role, and how can you prepare to navigate them with integrity?

2. *Building an Ethical Culture:*
   As a leader, how are you promoting ethical behavior within your organization? Are there areas where your team might be cutting corners or prioritizing short-term gains over long-term ethical standards?

   What steps can you take to foster a culture of transparency, accountability, and ethical responsibility in your organization?

3. *Long-Term Ethical Leadership:*

   Do your current business practices align with your long-term ethical goals? Are you making decisions today that will positively impact your organization's future and the people it serves?

   How can you integrate ethical decision-making into your long-term strategy for success?

4. *Ethics in Healthcare:*

   As a healthcare executive, how are you balancing financial responsibility with the ethical obligation to provide high-quality patient care? What systems do you have in place to ensure that ethical considerations are at the forefront of your decision-making?

   How can you promote equitable access to care in your healthcare organization, and what challenges do you anticipate in addressing disparities?

Final Thoughts: Leading with Integrity

The desire and practice of ethical leadership is the determined focus on building a foundation of trust, transparency, and responsibility that permeates every level of your organization. Whether you're steering a startup, a Fortune 500 company, or a healthcare system, your legacy will ultimately be defined by the ethical choices you make. By leading with integrity, you can create a lasting positive impact on your organization, your community, your colleagues, your employees, and ultimately, the people you serve.

Obiter Dictum:

Integrity is not a theoretical concept in leadership; it is operational. In the boardrooms I have led and the systems I have helped to stabilize, ethics have never been a soft concept. They are the hard lines you maintain when compromise feels convenient. The difference between good and great leadership often rests on how you act when no one is watching. If you want enduring trust, make sure every decision, whether public or private, reflects your highest principles. Because at the end of the day, your leadership legacy will not be remembered for quarterly results, but for the values you defended when they were hardest to uphold. Leadership is never short on complex decisions but when values lead, the path becomes clearer.

Scenario:

You uncover a questionable practice embedded in your company's operations.

What Would a Worthy Roman Imperator Do?

Follow Cicero's path: Speak truth to expose wrongdoing and questionable actions. Defend justice even at personal risk. Leadership without integrity is no leadership at all.

Ethics build trust, but the crucible of leadership is crisis. When the world tilts and uncertainty reigns, the leader must not only stand but hold the line. What does Roman resilience teach us about leading in turbulent times?

"To rule oneself is the ultimate form of power."

–Seneca

CHAPTER V

Holding the Line: Fortitude at the Frontiers

Focus: Strategic leadership emerges in times of crisis.
This chapter explores the strength of stabilizing
forces and the wisdom of timely restraint.

E very organization, whether a business or a healthcare system, will face crises. These challenging time periods, whether a sudden economic downturn, a global pandemic, or an internal challenge like losing a key leader, provides a key juncture for any company. While catastrophes can threaten to derail operations, they also present leaders with the opportunity to demonstrate resilience, strategic foresight, and adaptability. History shows us that great leaders emerge stronger from crises, and today's entrepreneurs and executives must cultivate the ability to steer through turbulent times with vision and clarity.

In this chapter, we'll explore how ancient and modern leaders have successfully navigated crises, and how their lessons are directly relevant for today's business and healthcare executives. You'll learn how to balance short-term responses with long-term planning, how to maintain morale during tough times, and how to use crises as catalysts for innovation and transformation.

Emperor Hadrian

Hadrian (117–138 AD) was the emperor who knew when to say, "Let's stop conquering for a moment and get our house in order." Following the expansive reign of his predecessor, Trajan, Hadrian focused on consolidation rather than conquest. This decision cemented his reputation as one of Rome's most strategic leaders. His reign was marked by a determination to focus on stability and solidify the empire in order to govern it well.

Hadrian's Wall: A Masterclass in Strategic Boundaries

Hadrian's most famous legacy, *Hadrian's Wall*, was designed to be more than a defensive structure alone. It was built in northern Britain to mark the edge of the Roman Empire, the wall stretched over 70 miles, complete with forts, guard posts, and milecastles. It symbolized Rome's commitment to stability and order. The wall was built to keep barbarians out, control movements, secure resources, and send a clear message: *This is Rome's border, and we're here to stay.*

Hadrian understood that good leadership sometimes means knowing when to stop expanding and instead focus on fortifying what you have. Modern leaders can take a page from his playbook by recognizing when to prioritize internal strength over external growth.

A Diplomatic Emperor

Hadrian built walls, and he built relationships. A lover of Greek culture, he traveled extensively across the empire, visiting nearly every province. He made a choice not to rule from a distant palace in Rome. He met his people where they were, learning their customs and earning their loyalty. Hadrian fostered cultural integration, blending Roman traditions with local practices to create a sense of unity across diverse regions.

For leaders who manage diverse teams or global organizations, Hadrian's approach is a reminder that meeting people on their terms fosters trust and collaboration. His ability to navigate cultural differences made him one of Rome's most adaptable emperors.

Hadrian the Visionary

Beyond his wall, Hadrian's architectural legacy includes the Pantheon, one of the most iconic buildings in Rome. Its massive dome, still the largest unreinforced concrete dome in the world, symbolizes his ability to think big, both literally and figuratively. While he focused on stability, Hadrian never stopped innovating.

Lessons for Modern Leaders

Know when to consolidate. Hadrian's decision to stabilize the empire rather than expand it shows that good leadership isn't always about charging ahead. Sometimes, wise leadership is about taking stock, reinforcing strengths, and addressing vulnerabilities.

Engage with your people. By traveling throughout the empire, Hadrian ensured his leadership was visible and relatable. Leaders today can replicate this by staying connected to their teams, even in large organizations.

Balance defense with innovation. Like Hadrian's Wall and the Pantheon, strong leaders protect what matters while remaining open to new ideas and possibilities.

Legacy Beyond Borders

Hadrian's reign is a testament to the power of thoughtful, deliberate leadership. His ability to balance strategy, diplomacy, and innovation created an empire that could weather storms long after he was gone. The next time you're faced with a challenge, ask yourself: *What would Hadrian do?*

Emperor Vespasian

When Vespasian (9–79 AD) took the throne, Rome was in shambles. The chaos of the *Year of the Four Emperors* (69 AD) had left the empire politically fractured and financially drained. Nero's lavish spending had emptied the treasury, and trust in leadership was at an all-time low. Enter Vespasian: a no-nonsense leader who brought stability, restored order, and proved that a little pragmatism can go a long way.

Rebuilding Rome's Finances

One of Vespasian's first acts was to replenish the treasury. His approached proved he wasn't shy about how he did it. He introduced new taxes, including one on public toilets, which led to the famous phrase, "Money doesn't stink" (*pecunia non olet*). It was classic Vespasian: practical, unapologetic, and focused on results.

Though his methods raised eyebrows, they worked. Vespasian's financial reforms laid the groundwork for long-term stability, proving that sometimes leadership means making tough, unpopular decisions for the greater good.

The Colosseum: A Symbol of Unity

Vespasian focused on fixing Rome's finances while also giving the people something to rally around. He initiated construction of the Flavian Amphitheater, better known as the Colosseum, turning Nero's extravagant private palace into a public space for entertainment. The message was clear: *Rome belongs to the people, not the elite.*

The Colosseum served not just as an architectural marvel but also as a visible unifying symbol for a divided empire. Leaders today can learn from this by finding ways to bring their teams together around shared goals and values.

A Man of the People

Vespasian was known for his humor and relatability. He didn't take himself too seriously, often joking about his mortality. On his deathbed, he quipped, "Oh dear, I think I'm becoming a god." His wit humanized him, making him a leader the people could relate to and trust.

Lessons for Modern Leaders

Stabilize first, innovate later. Like Vespasian, focus on addressing immediate crises before chasing ambitious goals. Rebuild trust, secure resources, and ensure your foundation is solid.

Create unity through shared symbols. The Colosseum brought Romans together. Leaders today can create similar cohesion by fostering shared values, traditions, or initiatives that resonate across teams.

Stay relatable. Vespasian's humor and pragmatism made him approachable, reminding leaders that authenticity builds trust.

Legacy of a Pragmatist

Vespasian wasn't flashy, but he didn't need to be. His practical approach to leadership turned a chaotic empire into a stable one, proving that sometimes the best leaders are the ones who focus on the basics. If you're ever faced with a seemingly insurmountable challenge, channel your inner Vespasian: roll up your sleeves, make the hard calls, and maybe share a humorous anecdote or two along the way.

Emperor Diocletian

When Diocletian (244–311 AD) took power in 284 AD, the Roman Empire was in crisis. Plagued by political instability, economic decline, and external threats, Rome seemed destined to fall. Diocletian's solution? A complete overhaul of the system.

The Tetrarchy: Power in Numbers

Diocletian realized that one man couldn't effectively govern an empire as vast as Rome. His answer was the Tetrarchy, a system that divided the empire into four regions, each ruled by a co-emperor or deputy. This innovative structure allowed for faster responses to crises and more localized governance.

Economic and Military Reforms

Diocletian did not stop at political reform. He introduced price controls to combat inflation, reorganized the tax system, and strengthened the military. His reforms weren't always popular (especially the price controls), but they stabilized the empire during one of its most precarious periods.

Leadership Lesson: Diocletian's reign shows that bold, systemic changes can turn chaos into stability. Modern leaders can learn from his willingness to delegate authority and think outside the box.

A Legacy of Reinvention

Diocletian's reforms revitalized the empire, but his true legacy lies in his ability to adapt and innovate. He reminds us that when faced with overwhelming challenges, sometimes the best solution is to rewrite the rules entirely.

Crisis Leadership in Ancient Rome: The Calm in the Storm

The Roman Empire faced countless crises during its centuries of dominance, from external invasions to internal power struggles and natural disasters. How did it endure for so long? One of the key reasons was the strategic leadership exhibited by figures like Emperor Augustus and Marcus Aurelius. Their ability to manage crises while maintaining a clear vision for the future offers a lesson for any modern leader.

Augustus, Rome's first emperor, inherited a city ravaged by civil war. The Roman Republic had collapsed into chaos, and the future of the empire hung in the balance. Instead of reacting to the immediate crisis with short-term solutions, Augustus developed a long-term strategic plan to bring stability and growth to Rome. His reforms reshaped the military, revitalized the economy, and solidified political structures that ensured Rome's survival for centuries.

On the other hand, Marcus Aurelius, often called the philosopher-emperor, faced a different type of crisis. His reign was marked by nearly constant warfare, plague, and political intrigue. Yet, despite the challenges, he maintained a calm and measured approach. His famous work *Meditations* reflects a stoic philosophy that emphasizes the importance of focusing on what you can control, staying calm in adversity, and maintaining a sense of ethical duty.

For entrepreneurs and executives today, these leaders offer

powerful lessons: strategic thinking, a long-term vision, and emotional resilience are key to navigating crises.

Antoninus Pius: The Quiet Power of Preventive Leadership

Why Antoninus Pius? While many Roman emperors are celebrated for their conquests, Antoninus Pius was notable for avoiding conflict and focusing on the internal stability of the empire. His leadership was marked by peaceful diplomacy, fiscal responsibility, and careful governance. Rather than reacting to crises, he prevented them by focusing on fortifying the empire's borders, strengthening legal institutions, and investing in infrastructure such as roads and aqueducts.

For modern entrepreneurs and executives, Antoninus Pius teaches *create environments of stability strategically*, where organizations can thrive without unnecessary disruption, helps minimize dramatic and reactive decisions that can occur during crises and greatly harm a once prosperous organization.

Key Leadership Lesson from Antoninus Pius: Sometimes, the best leadership is *subtle* and *preventive*. Antoninus Pius demonstrated that *stability and foresight* are as valuable as bold decision-making in times of crisis. Leaders who can prevent crises through thoughtful, steady governance create conditions for long-term success.

Case Study Application: Antoninus Pius' approach mirrors the leadership of Tim Cook at Apple, who took over from Steve Jobs. Cook's leadership style is less dramatic but marked by careful governance, operational efficiency, and long-term vision. Under Cook, Apple has continued to thrive, maintaining stability and growth without needing radical upheaval. Like Antoninus, Cook prioritizes stability and foresight over reactionary measures.

Case Study I: Apple—Surviving the Brink of Collapse

In the mid-1990s, Apple was on the verge of bankruptcy. Its market share had plummeted, its product line was bloated, and its leadership was in disarray. It seemed like the iconic tech company might not survive the decade. Steve Jobs, who had been ousted from the company years earlier, returned as CEO in 1997. Rather than panicking or making reactionary changes, Jobs implemented a strategic vision that involved streamlining Apple's product line, cutting non-essential projects, and rebranding the company as an innovative leader in consumer electronics.

One of his first moves was to negotiate a deal with Microsoft, a partnership that provided Apple with the financial backing it needed to stay afloat. Jobs introduced new products such as the iMac and eventually the iPod, which set the stage for Apple's transformation into the world's most valuable company.

Empire of Influence Takeaway:

Resilience and strategic focus are essential in times of crisis. Jobs did not exhibit consternation or just react to the crisis, he responded by using it as an opportunity to streamline and focus on what truly mattered to Apple's future.

Leaders should use crises as *inflection points* to re-evaluate their organization's direction. When faced with a crisis, ask yourself: What is the core value we provide? What can we eliminate to refocus on that?

Apple's story is a testament to the power of calm, focused leadership during turbulent times. Instead of succumbing to panic, Jobs steered Apple back on course with a clear and visionary strategy.

The Balance Between Immediate Response and Long-Term Strategy

When crises hit, leaders often feel the pressure to act immediately—and in many cases, they must. But while addressing immediate concerns is important, it is equally crucial to maintain a long-term perspective. Too often, leaders get caught up in the "*firefighting mode*," where they only focus on solving immediate problems without thinking about the bigger picture.

Take, for example, the financial crisis of 2008. Many companies, particularly in the banking sector, reacted by slashing costs, laying off workers, and retreating from risky ventures. Some of these measures were necessary to survive in the short term. However, the companies that truly thrived were those that combined short-term actions with long-term planning.

One company that managed this balance well was Goldman Sachs. During the crisis, Goldman Sachs took steps to secure its financial position, but it also invested heavily in emerging markets and technology, laying the groundwork for future growth. As a result, while some financial institutions never fully recovered, Goldman Sachs emerged stronger and more resilient.

Empire of Influence Takeaway:

Don't get trapped in short-term thinking. Crises demand immediate action, but don't lose sight of your long-term vision. The decisions you make today should not only address the present crisis but also position your organization for future success.

Take a *balanced approach:* Deal with the urgent while planning for the future. In times of crisis, ask yourself: How can we use this situation to strengthen our position in the long term?

Emotional Resilience and Leadership in Crisis

Crises are not only challenges to your organization but also challenges to your leadership. One of the most overlooked aspects of crisis leadership is the *emotional resilience* of the leader. In turbulent times, your team will look to you for guidance, and your ability to remain calm, composed, and focused will have a direct impact on their performance.

Marcus Aurelius is a classic example of emotional resilience in leadership. During his reign, the Roman Empire was plagued by constant wars and a devastating epidemic known as the Antonine Plague, which wiped out a significant portion of the population. Rather than becoming overwhelmed, Marcus Aurelius relied on his Stoic philosophy to maintain emotional balance and perspective. He believed that while we cannot control external events, we can control how we respond to them.

In today's business environment, emotional resilience is equally important. Leaders who can remain composed in the face of adversity are more likely to make clear-headed decisions and inspire confidence in their teams. This does not mean suppressing emotions or denying them; it means *managing them effectively*.

Case Study II: Howard Schultz and Starbucks— Navigating a Leadership Crisis

In 2008, Howard Schultz, the founder of Starbucks, returned as CEO to guide the company through one of its most difficult periods. The financial crisis had severely impacted Starbucks' business, and the company was losing market share to competitors. Schultz's first step was to acknowledge the severity of the situation to his team and the public. Instead of pretending that everything was fine, he openly communicated the challenges Starbucks was facing.

Schultz's leadership was marked by *emotional transparency*; he didn't hide his concerns but used them to motivate his team. Under his leadership, Starbucks took difficult but necessary actions, including closing underperforming stores and refocusing on the core values that had originally made the company successful. Schultz's willingness to be open about the challenges allowed him to rally his team and refocus the company's mission.

Empire of Influence Takeaway:

Emotional transparency and resilience are key to leading through a crisis. Don't be afraid to acknowledge the difficulties your organization is facing. Use them as a motivator for action.

As a leader, you set the emotional tone for your organization. If you remain calm and focused, your team will follow suit. If you panic, your team will likely do the same.

Schultz's ability to stay grounded and honest during Starbucks' crisis helped the company bounce back and emerge stronger than ever.

Turning Crisis into Opportunity: The Power of Innovation

It is often stated that *necessity is the mother of invention.* Nowhere is that more true than in times of crisis. While crises can expose vulnerabilities, they also force organizations to innovate in ways that might not have been considered during normal times.

One of the most striking examples of innovation during a crisis is the rise of Airbnb. In the wake of the 2008 financial crisis, people around the world were struggling financially. Homeowners sought ways to supplement their income, and travelers were looking for cheaper accommodations. Brian Chesky, Joe Gebbia, and Nathan Blecharczyk, the founders of Airbnb, saw an opportunity to meet these needs by creating a platform where people could rent out their homes or spare rooms.

What began as a way for people to earn a little extra money quickly grew into a global phenomenon, disrupting the hotel industry and changing the way people travel. By addressing specific needs that emerged during the crisis, Airbnb's founders turned a moment of economic uncertainty into a massive success.

Empire of Influence Takeaway:

Crises can be *catalysts for innovation*. When resources are limited and traditional approaches no longer work, this is often the perfect time to think creatively and introduce new solutions.

As a leader, encourage your team to see *crises as opportunities*. Ask: What new problems have emerged, and how can we solve them in a way that creates long-term value?

The lesson from Airbnb is clear: even in the darkest of times, there is room for innovation. Leaders who can pivot and adapt during crises are often the ones who come out ahead.

Special Section for Healthcare Executives: Leading through Health Crises

Few industries face crises as regularly and with such high stakes as healthcare. Healthcare executives must navigate a complex web of clinical, operational, financial, and regulatory challenges, all while ensuring the well-being of patients and staff. The COVID-19 pandemic underscored the importance of strategic, resilient leadership in healthcare and highlighted the need for quick decision-making paired with long-term planning.

Crisis Communication: During a healthcare crisis, clear and transparent communication is vital. Healthcare executives must provide accurate, timely information to their teams, patients, and the public. This was particularly evident during the COVID-19 pandemic, where mixed messages and misinformation often led to confusion and mistrust.

> *Leadership Tip:* Establish a crisis communication plan that ensures all stakeholders receive consistent, reliable information. Be open about the challenges your organization is facing and ensure that your messaging reflects both short-term responses and long-term strategies for recovery.

Resource Allocation: In times of crisis, healthcare organizations are often forced to make difficult decisions about how to allocate scarce resources. Whether it is ICU beds, ventilators, or PPE, healthcare leaders must balance the immediate needs of today with the long-term sustainability of their organizations.

> *Leadership Tip:* Develop a framework for ethical decision-making that prioritizes patient care while considering long-term resource management. Engage a diverse team in these discussions to ensure that all perspectives are considered.

Building Resilience: The healthcare industry is prone to crises, from pandemics to natural disasters to financial pressures. Healthcare executives must focus on building *resilient systems* that can withstand these challenges. This includes investing in infrastructure, training staff to respond to emergencies, and ensuring that the organization has the financial flexibility to weather tough times.

> *Leadership Tip:* Use crises as opportunities to assess and improve your organization's resilience. Conduct post-crisis reviews to identify areas where your response could have

been stronger and invest in the systems and processes that will make your organization more adaptable in the future.

Supporting Healthcare Workers: One of the biggest challenges during healthcare crises is maintaining the morale and well-being of healthcare workers. The COVID-19 pandemic saw record levels of burnout among healthcare professionals. Healthcare executives must prioritize the emotional and physical well-being of their staff to ensure they can continue to provide high-quality care.

Leadership Tip: Implement programs that support the mental and emotional health of your staff. This could include providing access to counseling services, offering flexible work schedules, or creating spaces where healthcare workers can decompress and recharge.

Reflection Questions

1. *Balancing Immediate and Long-Term Strategy:*
    Reflect on a time when you were in "firefighting mode" during a crisis. Were you able to maintain a long-term perspective, or did you get caught up in the immediate challenges? What would you do differently next time?

    How can you better balance the need for short-term crisis management with your organization's long-term vision?

2. *Emotional Resilience in Leadership:*
    How do you typically respond emotionally to crises? Do you find it difficult to remain calm and focused, or do you thrive under pressure?

What strategies can you implement to improve your emotional resilience and set a positive tone for your team during challenging times?

3. *Using Crises as Opportunities for Innovation:*
    Think about a crisis your organization has faced. Were there opportunities for innovation that you missed? How could you have used the crisis as a catalyst for new solutions or business models?

    How can you create a culture where your team sees crises not as setbacks but as opportunities for creativity and growth?

4. *Healthcare-Specific Crisis Management:*
    As a healthcare executive, how do you prioritize clear communication during a health crisis? Do you have systems in place to ensure that your messaging is consistent and reliable?

    What steps are you taking to build resilience within your healthcare organization? How are you preparing your team for future crises, both operationally and emotionally?

Final Thoughts: Leading through Crisis with Strategy and Resilience

Crises are inevitable in both business and healthcare, but how leaders respond to them defines their success. The most effective leaders are those who remain calm, think strategically, and use crises as opportunities to innovate and strengthen their organizations. Whether you're an entrepreneur navigating market disruptions or a healthcare executive leading through a pandemic, your ability to balance short-term crisis management with long-term vision will determine the future of your organization.

By embracing resilience, emotional intelligence, and a strategic approach to crisis leadership, you can emerge from any storm stronger, more successful, and operating as a focused and clear-thinking leader.

Obiter Dictum:

In times of crisis, leadership does not mean that you have all the answers; however, it does mean that you stand as the leader to create stability and provide direction when others are uncertain. I have led teams through operational disruptions, public health emergencies, and deep financial challenges. The true leaders may not be the loudest, but they will be the ones who rise up and the take the action necessary to address the issue. They are the ones who stand strong by showing up, staying composed, and making strategic choices that serve the organization during and after the storm has passed. If your people feel safe with you at the helm, they'll move forward even in uncertainty. That is the true mark of fortitude, trust, and leadership.

Scenario:

A crisis strikes: public relations disaster, financial downturn, operational chaos.

What Would a Worthy Roman Imperator Do?

Stand firm like Hadrian at the frontier. Build defensive walls, stabilize your systems, and hold steady against the storm. Leadership is resilience under siege.

Amid a crisis, the temptation is to control. But Rome reminds us: true strength often lies in service. In the next chapter, we explore how humility, not dominance, secures lasting influence.

"To govern is to serve, nothing more and nothing less."

–Seneca

CHAPTER VI

Strength in Service: Humility in the Age of Empire

*Focus: Servant leadership isn't soft; it's foundational.
From ancient Rome to the modern boardroom,
true influence is built through lifting others.*

I n a world where leadership is often associated with power, ambition, and success, we can sometimes forget that the most impactful leaders are those who lead with *heart*. These are the leaders who put service and humility at the forefront of their actions. They truly recognize that real success is not only about what they achieve but also about the lives they touch and the positive impact they create in their organizations, communities, and industries.

This chapter delves into how today's entrepreneurs and executives can harness the power of *servant leadership*, focusing on how humility, empathy, and a commitment to service can transform teams, foster innovation, and create sustainable success.

By examining historical and contemporary examples of servant leaders, we'll explore how this leadership style remains as relevant and powerful today as it was centuries ago. The healthcare industry, with its inherent focus on service, offers unique opportunities for leaders to embrace these qualities.

The Essence of Servant Leadership: Putting Others First

The concept of servant leadership is not new; however, it is often overshadowed by our more aggressive, results-driven leadership styles. Robert K. Greenleaf, who popularized the term in the 1970s, defined servant leadership as a philosophy in which leaders prioritize the needs of their team, helping them grow and succeed, while promoting a greater sense of community and shared purpose.

In fact, we must return to ancient Rome and one of our earlier discussions, as it provides the earliest examples of servant leadership in the figure of Cincinnatus, the Roman farmer and statesman who was called upon to serve as dictator during a time of crisis. After successfully leading the Roman army to victory, he chose not to use his newfound power to enrich himself or extend his rule. Instead, he relinquished control and returned to his farm. His humility and commitment to the good of the people made him a lasting symbol of selfless leadership.

For today's leaders, the lesson is clear: *true leadership is focused on using the position's power to serve and uplift the many others around you. It must not be about wielding power for personal gain.* In an age where leadership is often measured by titles and accolades, servant leadership reminds us that the most profound impact comes from humility and service.

Case Study I: Herb Kelleher—Southwest Airlines and Servant Leadership

One of the most celebrated examples of servant leadership in the modern business world is Herb Kelleher, co-founder and former CEO of Southwest Airlines. From the beginning, Kelleher built Southwest Airlines on a foundation of putting employees first. His belief was simple: if you take care of your employees, they will, in turn, take care of your customers, and the business will thrive.

Kelleher was known for his humility, often going out of his way to engage with employees at all levels. Whether he was helping out with baggage handling or chatting with flight attendants, Kelleher consistently demonstrated that no job was beneath him. This not only fostered a sense of trust and loyalty among his employees but also created a culture where everyone felt valued and empowered.

Southwest's success, under Kelleher's leadership, was built upon an organization that valued people above profits, it was not merely clever business strategies or competitive pricing. It's foundation was the culture. By putting his employees first, Kelleher ensured that customers received exceptional service, which, in turn, drove the airline's profitability and growth.

Empire of Influence Takeaway:

Servant leadership fosters loyalty and long-term success. Kelleher's approach shows that when leaders prioritize the well-being of their teams, they build a culture of loyalty, trust, and excellence.

As a leader, ask yourself: how are you serving your employees? Do they feel valued, empowered, and trusted? The way you treat your team will be reflected in how they treat your customers and, ultimately, your business's bottom line.

Humility as a Leadership Superpower

Humility is often misunderstood in the world of leadership. Many people assume that humility means being passive or weak, but in reality, humility is a form of strength. A humble leader acknowledges his or her limitations, seeks input from others, and is open to learning and growth. By putting one's ego aside, humble leaders create space for innovation, collaboration, and authentic relationships within their teams.

Let's consider the example of Satya Nadella, the CEO of Microsoft. When Nadella took over the helm in 2014, Microsoft was rapidly losing relevance in an evolving tech landscape. The company was seen as a rigid, top-down organization struggling to innovate. Nadella, known for his humility and empathy, embarked on a mission to transform Microsoft's culture.

Rather than asserting his own vision without input, Nadella encouraged a culture of *learning and collaboration*. He empowered his teams to think creatively and take risks, which led to breakthroughs in cloud computing and artificial intelligence. Under his leadership, Microsoft regained its status as a tech leader, with its market value more than tripling during his tenure.

Nadella's humility was not only a personal trait, but also it became a cornerstone of Microsoft's resurgence. By leading with humility, he created a culture where employees felt empowered to innovate, take risks, and contribute to the company's success.

Empire of Influence Takeaway:

Humility fosters innovation. Leaders who are humble recognize that they don't have all the answers, which creates an environment where others feel comfortable sharing their ideas and expertise.

As a leader, how can you practice humility? Are you willing to admit when you're wrong, ask for help, or give credit to others? By doing so, you can create a culture of collaboration and continuous improvement.

Case Study II: Mahatma Gandhi—Leading through Humility and Service

Few figures in history embody servant leadership as fully as Mahatma Gandhi. Even with his deep commitment to justice, Gandhi's leadership was not built on power or authority. It was firmly established on *service and humility*. He led by example, practicing the values he preached, and demonstrating that leadership is about serving the greater good rather than one's own self-interest.

Gandhi's philosophy of nonviolent resistance was rooted in his belief that ethical leadership required humility and a willingness to suffer for a greater cause. He never sought personal glory or power, and his life was a testament to the idea that leaders are servants of the people they lead. His leadership played a pivotal role in India's struggle for independence, inspiring millions to fight for justice and freedom.

Empire of Influence Takeaway:

Leadership is about service, not power. Gandhi's example reminds us that leadership is not about exerting control over others, it's about serving them. In business, this means putting the needs of your customers, employees, and community above personal gain.

Ask yourself: as a leader, are you focused on your own success or the success of those you lead? True leadership requires you to prioritize the well-being of others, even when it means personal sacrifice.

The Importance of Empathy in Leadership

Empathy is a critical component of servant leadership. Empathetic leaders are able to understand and connect with their teams on a deeper level, fostering trust, collaboration, and loyalty. *Empathy is a powerful tool for building strong, cohesive teams that can intellectually and emotionally overcome challenges, together.*

Case Study III: Dr. Ruth Pfau— A Modern Healer with an Ancient Heart

Dr. Ruth Pfau (1929–2017) was a German Pakistani physician and Catholic nun who dedicated over 55 years of her life to eradicating leprosy in Pakistan. Arriving in Karachi in 1960 to fix a visa issue en route to India, she encountered leprosy patients living in devastating conditions and made an immediate decision to stay.

What followed was a lifetime of service rooted in humility, compassion, and system-level transformation. Pfau worked with the government, military, local NGOs, and religious organizations to build a network of over 150 leprosy treatment centers across Pakistan, from bustling cities to remote mountain villages.

Dr. Pfau's work exemplifies the *Roman leadership principle of cura publica*, care for the public while modeling what it looks like to lead with heart, not ego. She was compassionate, yes, but also *strategic, resilient, and systemic* in her leadership. Like the servant leaders of ancient Rome (think Cincinnatus or Cornelia Africana), she operated without regard for personal glory, focusing instead on sustainable public good.

When Dr. Pfau began treating leprosy patients in Pakistan in the 1960s, she realized that medicine alone wasn't enough. Many of the afflicted were outcasts, feared and stigmatized. Pfau's approach was deeply holistic: she treated both the disease and the isolation.

She personally trained doctors and nurses, advocated for patient reintegration into society, and designed mobile clinics to serve remote areas. By 1996, thanks in large part to her efforts, the World Health Organization declared leprosy under control in Pakistan, the first country in the region to achieve this milestone.

Her compassion did not stop with healthcare. She advocated for education, dignity, and equality, working with communities to reshape attitudes toward disease and suffering.

Pfau's success came from building bridges and connecting with others who were reluctant or unable in the past to address these concerns. She partnered with the Pakistani government, working through shifting political regimes, economic instability, and cultural resistance. Her credibility came not as a result of status, but from her consistency, humility, and presence.

She refused special treatment. She lived modestly and worked directly in the field, often sleeping in leprosy colonies and traveling by jeep through dangerous terrain to reach patients others had forgotten. Dr. Ruth Pfau received Pakistan's highest honors including the Hilal-i-Imtiaz and Nishan-i-Quaid i Azam and eventually became a naturalized citizen. After her death in 2017, she was given a state funeral with full honors, the first Christian woman to receive such distinction in Pakistan.

Her leadership was quiet, faithful, and profoundly transformative. It was the kind of legacy that Rome itself would have revered.

This spirit of partnership echoes the collaborative leadership of Roman figures like Antoninus Pius, who governed not through domination but *through trust and moral authority.*

Empire of Influence Takeaway:

Empathy strengthens leadership. Leaders who can put themselves in others' shoes are better able to understand the needs and concerns of their teams, which leads to stronger relationships and better outcomes.

Lead through presence. Pfau believed leadership began by "showing up"—physically, emotionally, and consistently. Leaders who work shoulder-to-shoulder with their teams, especially in hardship, earn a different kind of trust.

Build systems, not spotlights. Her legacy lives in institutions, not headlines. She focused on *training others and building infrastructure,* ensuring care would continue long after she was gone.

Redefine success. For Pfau, success wasn't eradicating a disease; it was *restoring human dignity.* She believed health was not just physical, but social and emotional too.

Consider how you can practice empathy in your leadership. Are you taking the time to listen to your employees' challenges and concerns? How can you create a culture where people feel seen and heard?

Case Study III: Tim Cook—Leading Apple with Empathy and Service

When Tim Cook succeeded Steve Jobs as CEO of Apple, many wondered whether he could fill the shoes of one of the most iconic leaders in business history. Cook, however, took a different approach to leadership than Jobs. While Jobs was known for his visionary but demanding leadership style, Cook's leadership has been defined by *empathy, humility, and a commitment to service.*

Under Cook's leadership, Apple has continued to thrive, but the company's culture has also evolved. Cook is known for his *open-door policy*, his willingness to listen to employees at all levels, and his emphasis on inclusivity and diversity. He has also led Apple in adopting more ethical practices, such as improving working conditions in its supply chain and becoming a leader in sustainability.

Cook's focus on empathy and service has made Apple a more ethical company. Furthermore, his approach has strengthened Apple's brand and solidified its place as a leader in the tech industry.

Empire of Influence Takeaway:

Empathy and humility are not signs of weakness; they are the foundation of strong leadership. Cook's leadership shows that by putting people first, leaders can build organizations that are both successful and socially responsible.

How can you incorporate empathy into your leadership style? How can you ensure that your decisions reflect a genuine concern for the well-being of your employees, customers, and the broader community?

Servant Leadership and Innovation: The Ripple Effect

Leaders who embrace humility and service create cultures that are more innovative, resilient, and adaptable. When employees feel supported and empowered by their leaders, they are more likely to take risks, share ideas, and collaborate. This creates a *ripple effect*, where servant leadership fosters a culture of trust and innovation that benefits the entire organization.

Let's look at Chick-fil-A, a company known for its focus on servant leadership. Dan Cathy, CEO of Chick-fil-A, believes that great leaders must be willing to serve those they lead. He has been known to visit restaurants to work alongside employees, whether it's cleaning tables or interacting with customers. This approach has created a culture of respect, where employees feel valued and empowered to deliver exceptional service.

Chick-fil-A's focus on servant leadership has also contributed to its success as one of the most profitable fast-food chains in the U.S., despite being open only six days a week. By prioritizing employees' well-being and encouraging service at every level, Chick-fil-A has built a loyal customer base and fostered innovation in customer service.

Empire of Influence Takeaway:

Servant leadership creates a ripple effect. When leaders prioritize service and humility, it inspires employees to do the same. This leads to higher levels of innovation, customer satisfaction, and long-term success.

As a leader, how can you create a culture of service and humility within your organization? How can you ensure that these values are reflected in the way your team interacts with customers and each other?

Special Section for Healthcare Executives: Servant Leadership

Healthcare is, at its core, a service-oriented industry. Yet, healthcare leaders often find themselves focusing on operational efficiency, financial performance, and regulatory compliance, sometimes at the expense of patient care and staff well-being. *Servant leadership* offers healthcare executives a framework for balancing the business side of healthcare with the core mission of serving patients and supporting healthcare providers.

Prioritizing Patient-Centered Care: Servant leadership in healthcare means putting patients at the center of every decision.

This goes beyond providing high-quality clinical care. It is our utmost responsibility to ensure that patients feel heard, respected, and cared for on an emotional level.

> *Leadership Tip:* Engage with patients and their families to understand their needs and experiences. Implement feedback mechanisms that allow patients to share their thoughts and ensure that their feedback informs your decision-making process.

Supporting Healthcare Workers: Healthcare executives must also prioritize the well-being of their employees. Healthcare workers often experience intense levels of stress, burnout, and emotional exhaustion. Servant leaders can support their staff by providing resources for mental health, creating a positive work environment, and fostering a culture of respect and collaboration.

> *Leadership Tip:* Establish programs that support the mental and emotional health of your staff. Regularly check in with your employees to understand their challenges and ensure that they feel supported and valued.

Building a Culture of Service: Servant leadership is about creating a culture where everyone, from frontline staff to executives, is focused on serving others. In healthcare, this means fostering a sense of shared purpose and ensuring that every member of the team is aligned with the organization's mission to provide compassionate, high-quality care.

> *Leadership Tip:* Regularly communicate the organization's mission and values to all staff members. Create opportunities for collaboration and team building to ensure that everyone feels connected to the organization's larger purpose.

Reflection Questions

1. *Practicing Humility:*
   Reflect on a time when you led with humility. How did it impact your team's performance and morale? What steps can you take to make humility a more consistent part of your leadership style?

   Are there moments when your ego gets in the way of leading with humility? How can you overcome these obstacles to create a more inclusive, collaborative environment?

2. *Leading with Empathy:*
   Think about a situation where you practiced empathy as a leader. How did it affect the outcome of the situation? In what ways can you integrate empathy more deeply into your daily leadership practice?

   How do you currently listen to your team members? Are there ways to improve how you gather feedback and act on their concerns?

3. *Creating a Culture of Service:*
   What are you doing to create a culture of service in your organization? Are your employees empowered to put the needs of others first, and do they feel supported in doing so?

   How can you inspire your team to embrace a mindset of service and humility? What systems or practices could you implement to foster this kind of leadership at every level of your organization?

4. *Servant Leadership in Healthcare:*

As a healthcare executive, how do you balance the operational demands of running a healthcare organization with the need to prioritize patient care and staff well-being?

How can you better support healthcare workers who are dealing with high levels of stress and burnout? What steps can you take to create a culture of compassion and respect within your organization?

Final Thoughts: The Power of Service and Humility in Leadership

Servant leadership may not always be the flashiest or most celebrated leadership style, but it is one of the most powerful. Leaders who put service, humility, and empathy at the forefront of their decision-making create lasting impact, not only in their organizations but in the lives of the people they serve.

Whether you're an entrepreneur building a startup, an executive running a global company, or a healthcare leader caring for patients, leading with heart is the key to building strong, resilient, and purpose-driven organizations. By prioritizing service and humility, you can create a culture where people feel valued, empowered, and motivated to achieve greatness together.

Obiter Dictum:

I will never forget leading through the early days of a major system-wide shift in healthcare delivery. It felt like Rome during its most uncertain moments, pressured from all sides; the local market uncertainty, national pressure, insurance payment challenges, competitors, and independent physicians, to name a few; nevertheless, what guided us through was not a reactionary response, it was the calm, focused, strategic patience we chose to uphold.

Over my years in executive leadership, especially in healthcare, real power resides in the ability to listen, to serve, and to support those doing the hard work on the floors, in the clinics, and serving face to face with the patient. During crises or calm, humility and service are the quiet forces that stabilize an organization. When leaders model this behavior, it ripples through the culture.

Ask yourself: Am I building a system around me, or through me? The latter always endures longer and leaves a legacy worth remembering.

Scenario:

Your frontline struggles under crushing pressure, morale is slipping.

What Would a Worthy Roman Imperator Do?

Invoke Cincinnatus: Step into the trenches. Serve first, lead always. Earn loyalty not through rank, but through humility and action.

Service builds unity; unity builds structure. As we lift others, we begin to build beyond ourselves. With humility as our foundation, we are called to construct systems that endure beyond our names.

*"A structure must be built to withstand both the
assaults of men and the ravages of time."*

–Vitruvius

CHAPTER VII

Builders of the Future:
Trajan's Blueprint for Legacy

*Focus: Transformational leaders not only address and
solve problems—they build resilient systems. This
chapter explores scalable models and lasting design.*

In leadership, there's a difference between achieving
success today and building something that lasts for
generations. While many leaders focus on immediate wins,
hitting quarterly targets or launching the next big product,
transformational leaders think beyond the short term. They build
systems, cultures, and organizations that endure long after their
tenure is over. These leaders recognize that true success comes from
creating a legacy that transcends their personal contributions,
empowering future generations to build on their work.

In this chapter, we'll explore the principles of *transformational
leadership*, examining how historical figures and modern executives
alike have built systems that last. Whether you're an entrepreneur
looking to scale your startup or an executive aiming to reshape

your organization for the long haul, this chapter will provide actionable insights into how to create sustainable, long-term success.

Trajan, or Marcus Ulpius Nerva Traianus, didn't earn the title *Optimus Princeps* (Best Emperor) for sitting around in a toga. He was a man of action, a general, a builder, and a leader who understood that Rome's greatness depended on strong foundations. Under his reign (98–117 AD), the Roman Empire reached its maximum territorial extent, stretching from modern-day Scotland to the Middle East. Yet, Trajan's true brilliance wasn't just in conquering new lands but in ensuring the empire had the infrastructure to support them.

The Builder Emperor

Trajan's reign is best remembered for his dedication to public works and infrastructure. His motto seemed to be: *If it's worth doing, it's worth over-engineering.* One of his crowning achievements was *Trajan's Forum*, an architectural marvel that served as a hub for trade, politics, and administration. Built with funds from his Dacian campaigns (modern-day Romania), the forum included a massive market, libraries, and the iconic *Trajan's Column*. This marble masterpiece is an incredible, 100-foot-tall comic strip, spiraling with carved scenes of his military victories. Think of it as the ancient Roman version of a blockbuster movie poster.

The *Trajan's Market*, often considered the world's first shopping mall, was another stroke of genius. Imagine a bustling complex where merchants sold everything from fine wine to splendid silks. Trajan's projects were not only incredibly practical, but also visionary. They connected people, fostered commerce, and showcased Rome's cultural and economic dominance.

Military Prowess Meets Visionary Leadership

Trajan wasn't just about bricks and mortar; he was also a military powerhouse. His conquest of Dacia was a strategic move to secure vital resources like gold. Ultimately, his subjugation expanded Rome's borders and allowed these key resources to fund many of his public works projects. This created a cycle where military victories fed economic growth and civic improvements. For Trajan, war was about glory and building a better Rome for the empire and the people.

But what made Trajan a great leader was not his ability to swing a sword; it was his understanding of balance. He didn't expand recklessly. Instead, he focused on ensuring that every new conquest was integrated into the Roman system. Roads were built, laws were established, and resources were managed, ensuring that Rome's infrastructure could support its growing population.

The People's Emperor

What truly set Trajan apart was his relationship with the people of Rome. He was approachable, pragmatic, and genuinely concerned with public welfare. Ancient historian Cassius Dio praised him for being "a ruler who thought more of the people than of himself." He invested heavily in grain subsidies for the poor, public entertainment, and welfare programs, ensuring that Rome's citizens felt the benefits of his leadership.

Trajan also maintained good relations with the Senate. While he held ultimate authority, he respected the Senate's role, working with them to pass legislation and manage the empire. This balance of power made him popular among Rome's elite and its general population.

Lessons for Modern Leaders

Trajan's leadership style holds valuable lessons for today's executives. First, *build for the future.* Trajan's projects were designed to last centuries, a stark contrast to modern leaders who often focus on short-term gains. His vision for sustainable growth ensured that Rome's infrastructure could support its population long after his reign.

Second, *balance ambition with practicality.* Trajan was bold, but he wasn't reckless. He expanded the empire while ensuring it had the resources and systems to thrive. Modern leaders can emulate this by scaling their organizations responsibly, ensuring that growth is supported by strong foundations.

Lastly, *lead with empathy.* Trajan's genuine concern for his people made him a beloved figure. He understood that leadership is not merely about making decisions; however, it is about serving those who rely on you. Leaders today can take inspiration from Trajan's focus on public welfare, ensuring their teams feel valued and supported.

A Legacy Set in Stone

Trajan's reign left an indelible mark on Rome. His projects, from aqueducts to markets, were not for purposes of showing off, they were about creating a Rome that could endure. Even today, *Trajan's Column* stands tall in Rome, a testament to his vision, his victories, and his legacy. It isn't difficult to imagine Trajan looking down from wherever Roman gods reside, nodding in approval at the enduring impact of his reign. *Final Thought:* If you want your legacy to last, build like Trajan: with purpose, vision, and the courage to think long-term.

Septimius Severus

Septimius Severus (145–211 AD) rose to power during one of Rome's most challenging times. It was the chaotic year of 193 AD, when five different men claimed the imperial throne. Severus emerged victorious; nevertheless, instead of reveling in his success, he rolled up his sleeves and got to work reshaping the empire for the long haul.

Military Overhaul

Severus recognized that Rome's military was its backbone. He increased soldiers' pay, allowed them to marry (a previously forbidden practice), and expanded the army's size. His reforms boosted morale and loyalty, ensuring the military's strength for years to come. He famously told his sons on his deathbed: *"Enrich the soldiers and ignore everyone else."* While a bit cynical, it reflected his understanding that a stable military meant a stable empire.

Legal and Administrative Reforms

Severus was a general as well as a diligent reformer. He revamped the empire's legal system, increasing access to justice and streamlining governance. His administration was efficient and pragmatic, prioritizing order and stability over tradition.

Leadership Lesson: Severus teaches us that strong systems build resilient organizations. Modern leaders can follow his example by investing in the "backbone" of their teams, whether that's training, resources, or morale-boosting initiatives.

Building for the Future

Severus made a point of being a soldier, administrator, and ambitious monument builder. His architectural legacy includes the

Arch of Septimius Severus, a grand tribute celebrating his military victories. Like Trajan, Severus understood that physical structures could reinforce a leader's vision and legacy.

Final Thought: If you want your leadership to last, think like Severus: prioritize stability, build strong systems, and invest in the foundations of your organization.

The Essence of Transformational Leadership: Thinking Beyond the Present

Transformational leadership is rooted in the idea that not only are great leaders excellent problem solvers, but they are also outstanding visionaries. These leaders are focused on the present while continually anticipating the future. The result is the creation of systems that allow their organizations to thrive for years to come. This kind of leadership requires *strategic foresight*, a focus on building strong organizational cultures, and a commitment to developing leaders who will continue to drive the mission forward.

One of the earliest examples of transformational leadership comes from Ancient Rome, where once again, we turn to Augustus Caesar, the first Roman Emperor. He transformed the crumbling republic into a resilient empire. When Augustus took power, Rome had been weakened by years of civil war and political corruption. Yet, instead of simply restoring order, Augustus set about building the foundations for an empire that would last for centuries.

He restructured Rome's political institutions, stabilized the economy, and reorganized the military, creating a system that could endure long after he was gone. By doing so, Augustus led Rome out of a major crisis and built a foundation for the *Pax Romana.* His leadership of Rome began the 200-year period of relative peace and prosperity.

For today's entrepreneurs and executives, the lesson is clear:

true leadership is about building something that lasts. It's not enough to solve the challenges of today. You must be the type of leader to create the systems, cultures, and structures that will enable your organization to thrive in the future.

Case Study I: Walt Disney—Building a Legacy That Endures

Few business leaders have left a legacy as enduring as Walt Disney. When Disney founded his animation studio in the 1920s, his focus was not simply on the next cartoon or film. He was already envisioning building a world of entertainment that would last long after he was gone. Over the course of his career, Disney pioneered the art of animation, created iconic characters like Mickey Mouse, and transformed the entertainment industry with innovations like Snow White and the Seven Dwarfs, the world's first full-length animated feature.

But Disney's true genius lay in his ability to build a system that could continue innovating long after he was no longer at the helm. In the 1950s, Disney began planning Disneyland, a theme park that would bring his stories to life in a whole new way. He envisioned Disneyland as the first of many parks around the world, creating a global brand that would extend far beyond films and television.

Today, the Walt Disney Company is a multi-billion-dollar conglomerate that spans film, television, theme parks, ocean cruises, and more. Disney's legacy continues to thrive, thanks to the systems he put in place to foster creativity, innovation, and long-term growth.

Empire of Influence Takeaway:

Long-term thinking is essential for lasting success. Walt Disney's ability to think beyond the next film or project allowed him to build a brand that endures decades after his death.

As a leader, ask yourself: *Are you focused only on immediate successes, or are you building a system that will continue to grow and innovate after you're gone?* What steps can you take to ensure that your organization thrives in the long term?

Disney's story is a powerful reminder that transformational leadership requires a blend of *vision, innovation, and long-term planning.*

Building a Legacy of Resilience: Transforming Culture for the Future

Transformational leadership isn't just about creating systems; it is also about creating *cultures that can adapt and thrive* in the face of change. One of the key elements of lasting success is resilience: the ability of an organization to navigate challenges, innovate in the face of disruption, and continue to grow over time. Leaders who focus on building resilient cultures understand that while crises will come and go, a strong culture will carry their organization through.

Let's look at IBM, a company that has undergone multiple transformations over its more than 100-year history. Thomas J. Watson, who led IBM from 1914 to 1956, wasn't just focused on selling business machines; he was focused on building a company culture of innovation, customer service, and adaptability.

Watson understood that technology would continue to evolve, and he wanted to ensure that IBM could evolve with it. Under his leadership, IBM shifted from selling punch-card machines to developing the world's first mainframe computers. This focus on innovation, combined with a strong culture of customer service, allowed IBM to weather multiple technological revolutions—from the rise of personal computing to the era of cloud computing.

Even today, IBM continues to be a major player in the tech industry, thanks to the resilient culture and systems that Watson built.

Empire of Influence Takeaway:

Resilient cultures are the key to long-term success. Like IBM, organizations that build cultures of adaptability and innovation are better positioned to navigate change and thrive in uncertain times.

As a leader, how are you cultivating a culture of resilience within your organization? Are you encouraging innovation and flexibility, or are you focused on maintaining the status quo?

Watson's leadership at IBM shows us that *transforming culture* is just as important as transforming systems when it comes to building an organization that lasts.

Case Study II: Amazon—Jeff Bezos and the Power of Long-Term Vision

Few leaders exemplify transformational leadership as clearly as Jeff Bezos, the founder of Amazon. When Bezos launched Amazon in 1994 as an online bookstore, he had a long-term vision that extended far beyond selling books. From the very beginning, Bezos was focused on building a company that could evolve with changing consumer behavior and technology. His goal in creating an e-commerce platform was ultimately to transform it into a global ecosystem that could offer anything to anyone, anywhere.

Bezos' approach to leadership was characterized by *long-term thinking* and a willingness to make strategic bets that may not pay off for years. In the early 2000s, for example, Amazon launched Amazon Web Services (AWS), a cloud computing platform that would go on to become one of the company's most profitable divisions. At the time, investing in cloud computing seemed like a risky move, but Bezos' long-term vision paid off. Today, AWS is a multi-billion-dollar business that powers much of the internet's infrastructure.

Bezos also understood the importance of *reinventing Amazon's culture* to align with his long-term goals. He encouraged a culture of customer obsession, where every decision was made with the customer in mind. This focus on customer experience, combined with Bezos' willingness to invest in the future, has allowed Amazon to become one of the most valuable companies in the world.

Empire of Influence Takeaway:

Long-term vision requires patience and strategic risk-taking. Jeff Bezos' willingness to invest in cloud computing and other long-term projects demonstrates the importance of thinking beyond immediate results.

As a leader, ask yourself: *Are you making decisions based on short-term gains, or are you willing to invest in the future, even if it means taking strategic risks?*

Bezos' leadership at Amazon highlights the power of *long-term vision* and the importance of building a company that can continue to evolve and grow.

Empowering Future Leaders: The Legacy of Transformational Leadership

One of the most important aspects of transformational leadership is the *ability to empower others.* Leaders who build systems that last are focused on their organization's success and they are heavily invested in developing the next generation of leaders who can carry the organization forward. By mentoring, coaching, and empowering others, transformational leaders create a ripple effect that extends far beyond their own contributions.

One historical example of this is Mary Parker Follett, a pioneering thinker in the field of organizational theory and leadership. In the early 20th century, Follett emphasized the importance of *collaborative leadership* and the idea that leaders should not be authoritarian figures, but rather facilitators who empower their teams to achieve collective goals.

Follett's ideas were ahead of her time, and they laid the groundwork for modern leadership concepts like *empowerment, delegation, and servant leadership*. Her belief that leaders should focus on developing others, rather than simply exerting control, has influenced generations of leaders across industries.

Empire of Influence Takeaway:

Empowering others is key to building a lasting legacy. Leaders who focus on mentoring, coaching, and developing their teams create organizations that are more resilient and capable of long-term success.

As a leader, ask yourself: *How are you empowering the next generation of leaders in your organization?* Are you creating opportunities for others to grow, take risks, and lead?

Follett's ideas remind us that *leadership is not about control.* It must be about fostering an environment where everyone can contribute to the organization's success.

Case Study III: Indra Nooyi—Transforming PepsiCo for the Future

When Indra Nooyi took over as CEO of PepsiCo in 2006, the company was already a global leader in the food and beverage industry. But Nooyi wasn't content to simply maintain PepsiCo's position; she wanted to transform the company for the future. Her leadership was characterized by a focus on sustainability, health, and long-term growth, which allowed PepsiCo to evolve in response to changing consumer preferences.

Nooyi's signature initiative was "*Performance with Purpose*," a strategy that focused on balancing financial performance with social responsibility. Under her leadership, PepsiCo began investing in healthier products, reducing its environmental impact, and improving conditions in its supply chain. Nooyi understood that the future of the food and beverage industry would be shaped by consumer demand for healthier, more sustainable products, and she positioned PepsiCo to lead that transformation.

Empire of Influence Takeaway:

Transformational leadership requires a focus on sustainability and long-term growth. Indra Nooyi's leadership at PepsiCo demonstrates the importance of aligning financial performance with social responsibility.

As a leader, how can you balance short-term performance with long-term sustainability? Are you making decisions that will ensure your organization's success in the future, even as consumer preferences and market conditions evolve?

Nooyi's leadership at PepsiCo shows that *transforming an organization for the future* requires a commitment to sustainability and continuous innovation.

Special Section for Healthcare Executives: Building Sustainable Systems

Healthcare is an industry that is constantly evolving, driven by advances in technology, changes in regulations, and shifting patient needs. For healthcare executives, *building systems that last* is a matter of providing consistent, high-quality care that improves patient outcomes and meets the needs of future generations.

Placing the patient in the center and building the infrastructure around them to meet their needs is the foundation for providing world-class care and a system that lasts.

Sustainability in Healthcare Systems: Healthcare executives must focus on creating systems that can adapt to changing healthcare landscapes. This means investing in *infrastructure, technology, and people* that will allow your organization to thrive, even in the face of new challenges. Whether it's implementing electronic health records (EHR) systems, adopting telemedicine, or building partnerships with community health organizations, sustainable systems are key to long-term success.

> *Leadership Tip:* Regularly assess your organization's infrastructure and identify areas where you can invest for the future. Are your systems scalable? Are they equipped to handle future healthcare challenges like population growth, technological advancements, or changing patient demographics?

Building a Culture of Continuous Improvement: In healthcare, continuous improvement is essential for maintaining high-quality care. Healthcare executives should focus on fostering a culture where innovation, learning, and improvement are ingrained in every aspect of the organization. This could involve creating cross-functional teams to solve complex problems, encouraging staff to suggest improvements, or investing in leadership development programs.

> *Leadership Tip:* Create formal processes for gathering feedback from staff and patients. Use this feedback to drive continuous improvement and ensure that your organization is always evolving to meet the needs of its patients.

Developing Future Healthcare Leaders: One of the most important responsibilities of healthcare executives is to *develop future leaders* who can continue the work of building sustainable healthcare systems. By mentoring and coaching emerging leaders, you can ensure that your organization remains strong and capable of navigating future challenges.

> *Leadership Tip:* Create leadership development programs that give emerging leaders the skills and experience they need to take on greater responsibilities. Ensure that your leadership pipeline reflects the specialty requirements of the patients you serve.

Reflection Questions

1. *Building Systems for the Future:*
   Think about the systems you've built in your organization. Are they designed to last, or are they focused on short-term results? How can you ensure that the systems you put in place today will continue to provide value in the future?

   What investments can you make today, whether in technology, infrastructure, or people, that will strengthen your organization's ability to adapt and thrive in the long term?

2. *Fostering a Resilient Culture:*
   Reflect on the culture of your organization. Is it resilient and adaptable, or does it resist change? What steps can you take to create a culture that embraces innovation and continuous improvement?

How can you empower your team to take risks, experiment with new ideas, and drive the organization forward?

3. *Empowering Future Leaders:*
   Are you actively mentoring and developing the next generation of leaders in your organization? What more can you do to create opportunities for emerging leaders to grow and take on greater responsibilities?

   How can you create a leadership pipeline that reflects the diversity of the communities your organization serves?

4. *Sustainability in Healthcare:*
   As a healthcare executive, how are you building sustainable systems that can adapt to the evolving healthcare landscape? Are you investing in the technology and infrastructure that will allow your organization to provide high-quality care in the future?

   What steps can you take to foster a culture of continuous improvement in your healthcare organization? How can you empower your staff to drive innovation and improvement?

Final Thoughts: Transformational Leadership for Long-Term Success

Transformational leaders understand that true success is about building enduring systems, cultures, and organizations that last. The results must be achieved and striving for world-class performance with the focus and discipline for the future is key. Whether you're leading a startup, a global corporation, or a healthcare system, your legacy will be defined by the systems you create and the leaders you empower. By thinking long-term, fostering resilience, and investing in the future, you can build an organization that continues to thrive long after you are gone.

Obiter Dictum:

I have always believed that a leader's real value consists of the accomplishments achieved during their tenure, and also in what and who continue to thrive after they have stepped aside. I have seen leaders who focus only on the crisis of the day, and I have been fortunate to work for those who design with tomorrow in mind. The difference? Focus and discipline. Systems outlast charisma. Cultures outlast pressure. It is imperative that you build with a defined purpose, brick by brick, as did Trajan during his successful reign. This priority action will create a foundation that provides the culture and infrastructure that others can build upon for the ongoing future. That is the goal of every transformational leader: *not to be remembered, but to make remembering unnecessary.* A true legacy.

Scenario:

You are tasked with scaling an organization sustainably, but resources are tight.

What Would a Worthy Roman Imperator Do?

Channel Trajan: Build carefully, disciplined step by disciplined step. Focus on quality systems and scalable design. Emperors who built well ruled longer.

Even the most sophisticated systems fail without collaboration.

The Romans knew an empire cannot stand on brilliance alone. It thrives when voices rise together in a shared purpose. Let's now consider how unity multiplies influence.

*"Do as much as possible, and talk of
yourself as little as possible."*

–Sallust

CHAPTER VIII

One Empire, Many Voices: Senate, Legions, and the Strength of Unity

*Focus: Empires rise when many work as one.
This chapter explores the strategic power of
shared vision and collective leadership.*

L eadership is often portrayed as a solitary endeavor, with visionaries single-handedly steering organizations through rough waters. But the truth is that even the greatest leaders need teams to succeed. Collaboration is the cornerstone of successful organizations. Whether you're an entrepreneur launching a startup or an executive overseeing a complex organization, your success largely depends on your ability to harness the collective power of your team.

This chapter focuses on the critical role of *collaborative leadership* in today's world. It's about leading from within the group rather than above it, fostering a culture where teamwork, communication, and shared ownership are the norms. By studying real-life examples from business and healthcare, we'll explore how collaborative leaders inspire innovation, break down silos, and build stronger organizations.

The Collaborative Leader: A New Paradigm for Leadership

For centuries, leadership has been seen as a hierarchical, top-down model. In this model, leaders were the decision-makers, the strategists, and the people in control, while everyone else simply executed their vision. But as organizations become more complex, global, and interconnected, this traditional model continues to become outdated. Today's leaders must be *collaborators, facilitators, and enablers*, ensuring that every member of the team has a voice and a role in achieving success. There is enduring truth through shared power.

Ancient Rome provides us with interesting examples of this approach in leadership. While many Roman generals were known for their individual feats, numerous highlights of the empire were established and built through collaboration, not command alone.

In fact, we can return to the first Roman emperor Augustus to see this in action. His visionary success was built through empowering capable partners with clear missions and shared loyalty. The partnership and collaboration with his trusted military commander and engineer, Marcus Agrippa, allowed for the implementation and execution of many of Augustus's military and infrastructure ambitions. This included Agrippa's leadership in the critical naval battles (e.g., Actium), and the supervision of aqueducts and public buildings. Agrippa was deeply trusted.

Furthermore, not only was Augustus such a tactful and masterful propagandist that he was able to win over a war-weary populace, but he was also able to provide the appearance of the traditionalist Republic while acting out his autocracy. He cleverly preserved the illusion of senatorial power by involving them in governance, allowing smoother transitions and reduced resistance. In addition, through the shared pursuit and ultimate collaboration with the Roman diplomat Gaius Maecenas, Augustus was able to acquire his support, counsel, and ultimately approbation of the great writers such as Livy, Virgil, and Horace to provide enthusiastic commendation and praise for the new leadership and traditional way of life.

Julius Caesar and the First Triumvirate, shared power for mutual gain. This informal political alliance of Julius Caesar, Pompey the Great (leading general), and Crassus (wealthy businessman) allowed them to dominate the Roman politics by dividing resources and influence. In fact, Caeser gained military command in Gaul, Pompey received land for his veterans, and Crassus gained tax advantages. This collaboration among the three proved valuable, for a time.

Strategic coalitions, even among rivals, can unlock resources and momentum; however, they must be managed carefully and with continued aligned goals to prevent breakdowns.

In further exploration of Julius Caesar as a leader and collaborator, he famously shared the hardships of battle, addressed his troops as *comrades,* and regularly rewarded them with land, pay, and very pronounced recognition. His collaboration was strengthened by shared struggle and mutual respect. He provides the kind of example as a leader who walked alongside his legions and earned the type of loyalty that endured.

Emperor Hadrian took a broader approach. He traveled extensively throughout the empire. Surprisingly, this was rare for an emperor. He worked to strengthen ties with governors, building infrastructure, and integrating local customs. Emperor Hadrian demonstrated respect for many of the provincial cultures and invested in their development. His demonstrated collaboration across regions and cultures required listening, study, the honoring of local expertise while aligning with a common purpose.

Looking further ahead, one of the most celebrated partnerships in medical history came from two unlikely collaborators: Dr. Alfred Blalock and Vivien Theodore Thomas, a white surgeon and his assistant black laboratory supervisor. Together, they pioneered the first successful surgery to treat "blue baby syndrome," a congenital heart defect. Although Thomas faced systemic racism and a lack of formal medical education, Blalock recognized his brilliance and gave him a pivotal role in the surgical breakthrough. Their collaboration saved countless lives and changed the course of heart surgery forever.

For leaders and executives today, this story serves as a reminder that true innovation often comes from the collective efforts of a diverse team. Leaders who create an environment where everyone's contributions are valued, regardless of their position, are more likely to inspire breakthroughs.

Case Study I: Steve Jobs and Jony Ive—
Creative Collaboration at Apple

Steve Jobs is often celebrated as a singular visionary who transformed Apple into one of the most successful companies in the world. However, what's often overlooked is the critical role of Jony Ive, the designer behind many of Apple's most iconic products, including the iPhone, iMac, and iPod. While Jobs was the face of Apple, it was his collaboration with Ive that fueled much of the company's success.

Jobs and Ive had a unique partnership that was based on mutual respect and a shared commitment to perfection. Jobs had a deep understanding of what consumers wanted, while Ive had an unparalleled talent for design. Together, they pushed each other to create products that were not only functional but also beautiful. Their collaborative approach to product development allowed Apple to redefine entire industries.

But this collaboration didn't happen by chance. Jobs recognized that his genius alone wasn't enough to revolutionize the tech industry; he needed a creative partner who could bring his vision to life. Their partnership is a testament to the power of collaboration between leaders and creatives.

Empire of Influence Takeaway:

Collaboration fuels innovation. Steve Jobs may have been the visionary, but without Jony Ive's design expertise, Apple's iconic products may never have come to life.

As a leader, ask yourself: *Are you building collaborative partnerships within your organization?* Are you open to input and feedback from all members of your team, especially those who offer different perspectives?

Jobs' partnership with Ive is a reminder that *collaborative leadership* can foster deep, creative partnerships within your organization which can definitely lead to extraordinary outcomes.

Breaking Down Silos: Collaborative Leadership in Action

One of the biggest challenges that organizations face today is the presence of *silos.* Teams or departments that operate independently, often to the detriment of the larger organization, are termed silos. Silos can stifle innovation, slow down decision-making, and create inefficiencies, especially in large organizations.

A well-known example of breaking down silos comes from Ford Motor Company under the leadership of Alan Mulally. When Mulally became CEO in 2006, Ford was in dire financial straits. One of his first tasks was to break down the silos that existed between different departments. It was imperative that engineering, marketing, and manufacturing began to work together. They needed to be united around a common goal: saving the company.

Mulally introduced a collaborative management system where executives from all departments met regularly to share information, track progress, and solve problems together. Instead of working in isolation, leaders across the organization were now collaborating to make decisions and drive the company forward. This approach not only helped Ford survive the 2008 financial crisis without taking a government bailout, but it also set the company on a path to long-term success.

Empire of Influence Takeaway:

Breaking down silos creates agility and efficiency. By encouraging cross-functional collaboration, Alan Mulally transformed Ford's culture and helped the company navigate one of the toughest periods in its history.

Are there silos in your organization? How can you foster more collaboration between departments to drive innovation and efficiency?

Mulally's leadership at Ford demonstrates the power of collaborative leadership in breaking down barriers and driving collective success.

Case Study II: Google's Project Aristotle— The Science of Teamwork

In 2012, Google launched an internal study called Project Aristotle to determine what makes the perfect team. The researchers studied hundreds of teams across the company to identify which factors contributed to high performance. Interestingly, they found that the most successful teams weren't the ones with the smartest or most talented individuals. Instead, the best teams had one key ingredient: psychological safety.

Psychological safety refers to the belief that team members can share their ideas, questions, or concerns without fear of embarrassment or punishment. Teams that had high levels of psychological safety were more likely to collaborate effectively, take risks, and come up with creative solutions. Conversely, teams that lacked psychological safety were more likely to fall into groupthink or fail to innovate.

Google's research reinforced the idea that *collaboration thrives in environments where people feel safe to express themselves.* It takes more than simply placing smart people in a room together; a leader must continually strive to create a culture where everyone feels comfortable contributing, regardless of their title or expertise.

Empire of Influence Takeaway:

Psychological safety is critical for effective collaboration. Google's Project Aristotle shows that when team members feel safe to speak up, ask questions, and take risks, they are more likely to collaborate effectively and produce better results.

As a leader, how are you fostering psychological safety within your team? Are you creating an environment where people feel comfortable sharing their ideas, even if they might be unconventional or risky?

Google's findings highlight the importance of creating a *supportive, trusting environment* where collaboration can flourish.

Collaborative Leadership in Crisis: The COVID-19 Pandemic

The COVID-19 pandemic was an unprecedented crisis that required leaders across industries to collaborate like never before.

Hospitals, businesses, government and many other organizations had to work together to develop solutions rapidly. These partnerships, necessitated by healthcare, encompassed everything from vaccine development to supply chain management to public health communications.

One of the most remarkable examples of collaboration during the pandemic came from Pfizer and BioNTech, who partnered to develop one of the first COVID-19 vaccines. Despite operating in different countries and cultures, the two companies worked closely together, combining Pfizer's manufacturing capabilities with BioNTech's mRNA technology to produce a vaccine in record time. Their collaboration helped save millions of lives and paved the way for future partnerships in pharmaceutical innovation.

The pandemic also forced businesses to rethink how they collaborate internally and externally. Many organizations shifted to remote work, requiring new levels of communication and trust among teams. Leaders had to adapt quickly to the challenges of managing remote teams, ensuring that collaboration remained strong even in a virtual environment.

Empire of Influence Takeaway:

Crises require collaboration. The COVID-19 pandemic demonstrated that when organizations and leaders work together, they can achieve incredible results, even in the face of uncertainty and adversity.

How can you foster collaboration within your organization, particularly in times of crisis? Are you prepared to break down barriers and work across departments, industries, and even borders to solve complex problems?

The collaboration between Pfizer and BioNTech shows that crisis leadership is often collaborative leadership and that working together can lead to groundbreaking solutions.

Special Section for Healthcare Executives:
Collaborative Leadership

Collaboration is especially critical in healthcare, where patient outcomes depend on seamless teamwork between healthcare providers, administrators, and support staff. In recent years, healthcare organizations have increasingly recognized the importance of *interdisciplinary collaboration*, bringing together teams of doctors, nurses, specialists, and administrators to provide coordinated, high-quality care.

Interdisciplinary Teams in Healthcare: Healthcare executives must create environments where *interdisciplinary teams* can collaborate effectively. This means breaking down silos between departments and encouraging open communication between different areas of expertise. For example, integrating clinical and administrative staff into decision-making processes can help align financial and patient care goals.

Leadership Tip: Foster regular meetings and communication channels that encourage collaboration between different healthcare departments. Ensure that clinical, administrative, and operational leaders have a shared understanding of organizational goals.

Collaborating with External Partners: Healthcare leaders must also collaborate with external partners, including suppliers, insurers, and community organizations. The COVID-19 pandemic underscored the importance of these relationships, as healthcare systems worked with government agencies and pharmaceutical companies to provide care and develop treatments.

Leadership Tip: Build and maintain strong relationships with external partners, especially those who can provide critical resources in times of need. Collaboration with external stakeholders should be proactive, not reactive.

Empowering Healthcare Workers to Collaborate: Collaborative leadership in healthcare also means empowering front-line workers to share their insights and contribute to decision-making. Nurses, doctors, and support staff have valuable perspectives that can improve patient care and operational efficiency. Listening is key.

Leadership Tip: Create opportunities for front-line workers to participate in leadership meetings and contribute their ideas. Encourage an open-door policy where healthcare workers feel comfortable sharing their insights and suggestions with leadership.

———

Reflection Questions

1. *Fostering Collaboration:*
    Think about the teams you lead. Are they collaborating effectively, or are there silos that prevent information-sharing and innovation? How can you break down barriers and encourage more cross-functional collaboration?

    How do you, as a leader, promote open communication and psychological safety in your organization? Are your team members comfortable sharing their ideas, even if they might challenge the status quo?

2. *Collaboration in Times of Crisis:*
    Reflect on a time when your organization faced a crisis. How did collaboration, or the lack of it, impact the

outcome? What steps can you take to ensure better collaboration in future crises?

Are there external partners or stakeholders with whom you could collaborate to address complex challenges in your organization? How can you foster stronger relationships with these partners?

3. *Collaborative Leadership in Healthcare:*
    As a healthcare executive, how are you encouraging interdisciplinary collaboration between clinical and administrative staff? What can you do to ensure that all areas of your organization are working together toward a common goal?

    How can you better empower front-line healthcare workers to contribute their insights and ideas to leadership discussions? What systems or processes can you put in place to facilitate this?

Final Thoughts: The Power of Collaborative Leadership

Collaboration is the backbone of successful organizations. Whether you're leading a small team or a global corporation, your ability to foster collaboration will determine your success. Collaborative leaders create environments where people feel empowered to share ideas, take risks, and work together to solve complex problems. By embracing diverse perspectives, breaking down silos, and fostering a culture of open communication, you can harness the full potential of your team and achieve extraordinary results.

In today's fast-paced, interconnected world, *no leader can succeed alone*. The greatest achievements come from the collective efforts of individuals working together toward a shared goal. By leading with collaboration, you can build stronger teams, foster innovation, and create an organization that is resilient, adaptable, and poised for long-term success.

Obiter Dictum:

Over the course of my leadership journey, I have learned that unity and alignment are built on a foundation of *trust*. The most effective organizations I have seen and been a part of were not the ones with the best tools or the most talent; they were the ones where individuals trusted that their voice mattered. Collaboration must be more than a feel-good initiative; it must be a strategic imperative. When silos fall, when ego steps aside, when we listen more than we speak, that is when we lead. The pandemic taught us that we must adapt and it also reminded us that we are stronger and better when we partner and strive together. Unity must be cultivated intentionally, especially in high-pressure environments like healthcare. It is not titles or organizational charts that build empires, in the final analysis, it is relationships.

Scenario:

Your team is fragmented, vision diluted across silos.

What Would a Worthy Roman Imperator Do?

Unite like the Roman Senate at its best. Align diverse talents under shared purpose. Build consensus without losing decisive momentum.

Collaboration fuels progress, and compassion fuels meaning. After all, what is unity without humanity? In the following chapter, we look at how the heart of leadership can transform systems from functional to truly healing.

"The health of the people should be the supreme law."

–Cicero

CHAPTER IX

Healing with Honor: Compassion as a Leadership Imperative

Focus: Empathy is not a luxury; it is a leadership essential. This chapter reveals how emotional intelligence shapes lives, teams, and entire systems.

In an age when technology and data drive decision-making, it can be easy to overlook the *human side of leadership*. Yet, the most successful entrepreneurs and executives understand that *compassion* is not a weakness but a powerful tool for transformation. Compassionate leaders create strong bonds with their teams, foster loyalty, and build organizations where people are motivated to contribute their best.

This chapter explores the concept of *compassionate leadership*, illustrating how empathy and emotional intelligence can inspire innovation, resilience, and long-term success. Through real-world examples and historical insights, you'll learn how leading with heart can create more connected, empowered, and productive organizations. Whether you're a business leader or a healthcare executive, understanding the importance of compassion in leadership will help you build a team that is extremely successful, and deeply committed to your organization's mission.

Compassionate Leadership: More Than a Soft Skill

Compassionate leadership may sound like a soft skill in contrast to the hard, results-driven approach many leaders are accustomed to taking. But make no mistake: compassion is a *strategic advantage* in today's business environment. Leaders who show genuine concern for the well-being of their employees create stronger teams, foster deeper trust, and boost productivity. Compassionate leadership does not mean coddling your team or avoiding tough decisions; however, it does mean demonstrating empathy and understanding while still holding people accountable.

One of the earliest champions of compassionate leadership was Marcus Aurelius, the Roman emperor and philosopher. Marcus Aurelius is often remembered for his stoic philosophy, but beneath his stoicism was a deep empathy for his people. In his private journal, *Meditations*, he often reflected on the challenges of leadership and the need for patience, understanding, and kindness in dealing with others.

Despite leading Rome during one of its most difficult periods, a time of war and plague, Marcus Aurelius never lost sight of his responsibility to the people. His decisions were driven by a sense of duty and compassion, not personal gain. He believed that leadership was a service to the people, and that true strength came from humility, empathy, and a commitment to the common good.

For today's entrepreneurs and executives, Emperor Marcus Aurelius's example demonstrates that compassionate leadership is not a weakness. As the Emperor shows, compassionate leadership is a strength that can guide organizations through crisis and change.

Case Study I: Dr. Mona Hanna-Attisha— Healing Through Courage

"I did what any doctor would do, I told the truth." –Dr. Mona Hanna-Attisha

It started with a spreadsheet.

Not a press conference, not a protest, not a headline but raw data quietly gathered by a pediatrician in Flint, Michigan.

Dr. Mona Hanna-Attisha had been hearing whispers. Her colleagues were concerned. Parents were nervous. The water looked and smelled off. Something didn't feel right, and in medicine, when something doesn't feel right, you do not ignore it. You investigate.

What she found was devastating.

After reviewing blood tests from children in Flint, Dr. Hanna-Attisha discovered a staggering rise in levels of lead. A neurotoxin known to cause irreversible developmental harm, particularly in young children. The data clearly showed: Flint's water supply, changed by city officials to save money, had become toxic. The government denied the problem. And yet, the numbers didn't lie.

Now comes the question: What should she do?

Speaking out meant taking professional, legal, personal risk.

The city was defensive. The state was silent. No one wanted to hear that a major public utility had failed its people. But Dr. Hanna-Attisha knew that silence would mean complicity.

So she stood up. She spoke. She named the crisis. And she refused to back down.

In a now famous press conference, she publicly revealed her findings. The backlash was immediate. Officials tried to discredit her. She was called "an unfortunate researcher," "hysterical," and "misinformed." But she didn't retreat. She went back to her data, her team, and her unshakable commitment to her patients.

And then, slowly, the world began to listen.

Her work prompted national media attention, congressional hearings, and eventually, policy reform. Flint's water system was forced to come to terms with its failures. Emergency measures were taken. Dr. Hanna-Attisha became a national symbol of *moral clarity under pressure.* A clear reminder that in medicine, leadership requires more than just a diagnosis. It means *defiance in the face of injustice.*

Leadership Rooted in Empathy

What makes Dr. Hanna-Attisha's story so powerful because it is the science combined with her demonstrated public compassion. She viewed the children's charts as more than numbers, she saw names. Faces. Futures.

Her work consisted of much more than the public exposure. She helped establish programs to provide long-term developmental support for the children impacted. She raised awareness about the links between environmental policy and health. She became a strong voice not only for Flint, but for health equity everywhere.

"Public health is about people," she said. "It's about making sure the most vulnerable are seen, heard, and protected—especially when others look away."

Roman Parallel: A Modern Cincinnatus

As detailed earlier, Cincinnatus was called from his farm to serve as dictator during a time of war in ancient Rome. He led swiftly, decisively, and then returned to civilian life. Today, he still seen as a symbol of service, not power.

Dr. Hanna-Attisha embodies that same spirit: a professional pulled into battle not as a result of ambition, but by *necessity,* and a deep-rooted sense of justice.

Her courage did not appear brash or loud. It was steady. Confident. Relentless.

The kind of moral leadership that is not looking for applause, only the action necessary to address the issue and solve the problem.

Empire of Influence Takeaway:

Dr. Hanna-Attisha reminds us that *the heart of leadership is protection.*

True leaders do not wait for permission to do the right thing.

They step forward, and even if seemingly inconvenient, take the necessary action despite the danger or possible negative ramifications.

Building Trust through Compassionate Leadership

One of the most powerful outcomes of compassionate leadership is *trust.* When leaders demonstrate that they genuinely care about the well-being of their employees, they build trust that strengthens the entire organization. Employees who trust their leaders are more engaged, more committed, and more willing to go above and beyond in their roles.

Howard Schultz, the former CEO of Starbucks, understood the importance of trust in leadership. Schultz's leadership was deeply rooted in his belief that business should be about more than just profits, it should be about people. When Schultz returned to Starbucks as CEO in 2008, the company was facing significant challenges. The global financial crisis had taken a toll on the business, and Starbucks' rapid expansion had led to declining quality and customer satisfaction.

Instead of focusing solely on cost-cutting measures, Schultz made a bold decision: he temporarily closed 7,100 U.S. Starbucks stores to retrain baristas on how to make the perfect espresso. This move cost the company millions of dollars, but Schultz believed it was necessary to rebuild trust with both employees and customers. By investing in his employees, Schultz demonstrated that he valued their development and believed in their ability to restore Starbucks' reputation.

Schultz's compassionate leadership helped Starbucks recover from the crisis and set the company on a path to renewed growth. Today, Starbucks is known not only for its coffee but also for its strong corporate culture and commitment to employee well-being.

Empire of Influence Takeaway:

Trust is the foundation of a successful organization. By showing genuine concern for your employees' well-being and investing in their development, you can build trust that leads to higher levels of engagement and performance.

As a leader, consider how you are building trust within your team. *Are you making decisions that demonstrate your commitment to your employees' growth and well-being?*

Howard Schultz's leadership at Starbucks is a powerful example of how *compassion and trust can drive organizational success*, even in times of crisis.

The Role of Emotional Intelligence in Compassionate Leadership

At the heart of compassionate leadership is *emotional intelligence (EQ):* the ability to understand and manage your own emotions, as well as recognize and influence the emotions of others. Leaders with high emotional intelligence are better equipped to handle the complexities of leadership because they can connect with their teams on a deeper, more personal level.

A well-known example of a leader with exceptional emotional intelligence is Oprah Winfrey. Oprah's success as a media mogul and philanthropist is not merely the result of her business acumen; it is also a testament to her ability to connect with people on an emotional level. Throughout her career, Oprah has used her platform to share stories of vulnerability, resilience, and hope, fostering a deep sense of empathy and trust with her audience.

In her leadership role at Harpo Productions, Oprah cultivated a culture of emotional openness and support. She encouraged her team to bring their own uniqueness to work, creating an environment where people felt valued and understood. Oprah's emotional intelligence allowed her to lead with compassion, making her not only a successful business leader but also a beloved figure who inspires millions.

Empire of Influence Takeaway:

Emotional intelligence is key to compassionate leadership. Leaders who can connect with their teams on an emotional level build stronger, more engaged organizations.

As a leader, how are you developing your emotional intelligence? *Are you taking the time to understand the emotional needs of your team and respond with empathy?*

Oprah Winfrey's leadership shows that *emotional intelligence is a personal strength and an extremely valuable business asset* that can help provide leaders the additional insight to build more compassionate, successful organizations.

Case Study II: Dr. Paul Farmer—Compassionate Leadership in Global Health

Dr. Paul Farmer (1959–2022), the co-founder of "Partners In Health" (PIH), was a pioneer in bringing healthcare to underserved populations in countries such as Haiti, Rwanda, and Peru. His compassionate approach to healthcare was based on a belief that everyone, no matter their circumstances, deserved access to high-quality care. Farmer's work extended beyond medicine. He was an advocate for global health equity and human rights, and his leadership helped transform the field of global health.

Dr. Farmer is a prime example of how *compassionate leadership* can bring about significant change, even in the most challenging environments. He led by example, building strong relationships with the communities he served and inspiring a new generation of healthcare leaders to prioritize compassion in their work.

Key Lessons from Dr. Paul Farmer

Leadership through Service: Farmer's leadership was driven by his deep commitment to social justice and his belief that healthcare is a human right. His work demonstrated that leaders can create profound change by putting service to others at the center of their mission.

Empathy and Advocacy: He treated the diseases and did not limit his approach to the immediate need, but also moved to address the root causes of inequality, poverty, and lack of access to care. Farmer's compassion extended beyond individual patients to communities, understanding that the context in which people live has a direct impact on their health.

Transforming Systems: Through Partners In Health, Dr. Farmer and his team built healthcare systems in places where none existed, improving the quality of life for millions. His leadership showed that *compassion can be systematized,* creating institutions that embed empathy in their core mission.

Case Study Application: Dr. Farmer's leadership can be compared to modern executives in the nonprofit and healthcare sectors who aim to create sustainable, mission-driven organizations. His ability to *scale compassion* through *Partners in Health* illustrates how empathetic leadership can drive both organizational success and broader social impact.

Final Thoughts on Dr. Paul Farmer's Inclusion

Dr. Farmer's work with *Partners in Health* represents a powerful example of how compassion can drive systemic change. His story offers lessons not just for healthcare executives but for any leader seeking to create a positive, lasting impact by leading with heart.

Case Study: Dame Cicely Saunders—Founding the Hospice Movement with Compassion

Dame Cicely Saunders (1918–2005) was a British nurse, physician, and social worker who founded the modern hospice movement, revolutionizing care for terminally ill patients. Before Saunders, end-of-life care was often impersonal and lacking in empathy. She believed that every life, no matter how limited by illness, had value and dignity. Saunders introduced the idea of palliative care, combining emotional, spiritual, and physical care, focusing on improving the quality of life for the terminally ill and their families.

Her leadership was not only in founding hospice care, but also in creating a lasting impact beyond it. Her approach immensely altered how the world viewed death, inspiring many others to lead with empathy and compassion. Her legacy lives on through St. Christopher's Hospice in London, as well as the countless palliative care units worldwide that abide by her philosophy.

Key Lessons from Dame Cicely Saunders

Leading with Compassion: Saunders understood that leadership was more than managing operations, it required a unique approach of listening to patients and addressing their needs holistically. Compassion became the cornerstone of her leadership style.

Humanizing Healthcare: She fundamentally changed how healthcare providers approach terminal care, demonstrating that empathy and emotional intelligence are essential to high-quality care.

Cultural Transformation: Saunders created the hospice and palliative care movement, which led to a cultural shift in the medical community, advocating for better pain management, emotional support, and dignity at the end of life. This reflects how compassionate leadership can lead to systemic change.

Case Study Application: Dame Cicely Saunders' compassionate leadership can be compared to leaders in modern healthcare who are working to humanize patient care, such as Bernadette M. Melnyk, a leader in evidence-based nursing. Just as Saunders' leadership transformed the end-of-life experience, healthcare executives today must consider how to integrate compassion into all levels of care, from palliative care to acute treatment.

Special Section for Healthcare Executives: The Power of Compassionate Healthcare Leadership

Dame Cicely Saunders demonstrated that healthcare requires treating diseases and yet much more is necessary to address the whole person. The whole person means taking into account the factors emotionally, spiritually, and physically for prospering in greater health. For healthcare executives, this means fostering a culture where patients feel cared for in all aspects of their lives.

Leadership Tip: Healthcare leaders should champion *palliative care principles* in all areas of healthcare. By focusing on dignity and patient-centered care, they can improve not just the quality of care but the overall experience for patients and their families.

Empire of Influence Takeaway:

Compassionate leadership can transform the healthcare landscape. Saunders' emphasis on dignity and emotional care reshaped how healthcare professionals view end-of-life care and should inspire leaders across industries to consider how they can bring empathy into their organizations.

Are you leading with empathy and a focus on holistic well-being, like Dame Cicely Saunders? *How can you integrate emotional intelligence and compassionate care into your leadership practices?*

Reflection Questions

1. *Empathy in Leadership:*
   How do you ensure that empathy and compassion are at the forefront of your leadership style? Are you actively listening to the emotional and human needs of your employees, patients, or customers?

2. *Transforming Systems with Compassion:*
   Dame Cicely Saunders built a movement around compassionate care. How can you transform your organization by embedding compassion into its core mission?

3. *The Human Side of Leadership:*
    In what ways are you humanizing your organization's approach to leadership? Are you creating a culture where people feel valued, even in the most challenging moments?

Final Thoughts on Dame Cicely Saunders' Inclusion

Dame Cicely Saunders' pioneering work in hospice care is a perfect fit in this chapter because she exemplifies *compassionate leadership at the intersection of healthcare and human dignity*. Her story illustrates how leaders can transform entire systems by leading with empathy and emotional intelligence, creating an enduring legacy that prioritizes the *human aspect* of care. This makes her an excellent example for executives seeking to lead with heart in any field, but especially in healthcare.

Compassionate Leadership in Innovation and Growth

While compassion is often associated with empathy and support, it also plays a critical role in *driving innovation* and growth. Compassionate leaders are attuned to the needs of their customers and employees, allowing them to identify opportunities for improvement and innovation. By understanding the pain points of their stakeholders, compassionate leaders can create products and services that truly meet the needs of the market.

One company that exemplifies compassionate leadership in innovation is Patagonia, the outdoor apparel company known for its commitment to environmental sustainability. Yvon Chouinard, Patagonia's founder, built the company on the principle of caring for the planet and its people. Patagonia's *"Don't Buy This Jacket"* campaign, which encouraged consumers to buy fewer, higher-quality products to reduce environmental waste, was a bold example of compassionate leadership driving innovation.

By focusing on sustainability and responsible consumption, Chouinard created a brand that resonates with environmentally conscious consumers. Patagonia's commitment to environmental stewardship has not only helped the planet; it has also driven the company's success. Today, Patagonia is one of the most respected brands in the world. It is known for its integrity, innovation, and commitment to social and environmental responsibility.

Empire of Influence Takeaway:

Compassion drives innovation. By understanding and addressing the needs of their customers and the planet, Yvon Chouinard and Patagonia built a brand that stands out in the marketplace.

As a leader, how can you use compassion to fuel innovation in your organization? *Are you listening to the needs of your customers, employees, and the broader community, and using that insight to drive meaningful change?*

Patagonia's success shows that *compassionate leadership can lead to bold, innovative solutions* that resonate with consumers and drive long-term growth.

Special Section for Healthcare Executives: Compassionate Leadership

In healthcare, compassionate leadership is especially important because the stakes are so high. Healthcare leaders are responsible not only for the well-being of their teams but also for the lives of the patients they serve. Compassionate leadership in healthcare means creating an environment where both healthcare providers and patients feel supported, respected, and cared for in their lives.

Fostering Compassionate Care: Healthcare executives have the unique opportunity to influence the culture of compassion in their organizations. By prioritizing compassionate care, leaders can create a healthcare system that treats patients with dignity and respect. This means not only providing high-quality medical care but also addressing the emotional and psychological needs of patients.

> *Leadership Tip:* Encourage healthcare providers to take the time to connect with patients on a personal level. Create systems that allow for patient feedback and ensure that patient care is holistic, addressing both physical and emotional well-being.

Supporting Healthcare Workers: Compassionate leadership in healthcare extends to supporting healthcare workers, who often face high levels of stress, burnout, and emotional exhaustion. By showing empathy for the challenges that healthcare workers face, leaders can create a more supportive, resilient workforce.

> *Leadership Tip:* Implement programs that support the mental and emotional well-being of healthcare workers. This could include providing access to counseling services, offering flexible work schedules, or creating opportunities for peer support.

Leading with Emotional Intelligence: Emotional intelligence is critical for healthcare executives, who must navigate complex relationships with patients, providers, and other stakeholders. Leaders with high emotional intelligence are better equipped to handle the emotional demands of healthcare and to create environments where empathy and compassion thrive.

> *Leadership Tip:* Develop your emotional intelligence by actively listening to the concerns of healthcare providers and patients. Use this insight to inform decision-making

and create policies that prioritize compassionate care and employee well-being.

Reflection Questions

1. *Compassionate Leadership in Practice:*
   Reflect on a time when you demonstrated compassion as a leader. How did it impact your team and the outcome of the situation? How can you integrate compassion more consistently into your leadership style?

   Are there opportunities within your organization where you can show greater empathy and support? How can you create a culture that prioritizes compassion, both for employees and customers?

2. *Building Trust through Compassion:*
   How are you building trust with your team? Are your actions aligned with your commitment to their well-being and success? What steps can you take to strengthen the trust within your organization?

   How can you create an environment where people feel safe to express their concerns and challenges? How can trust be used as a foundation for stronger collaboration and innovation?

3. *Emotional Intelligence and Leadership:*
   As a leader, how do you manage your own emotions, especially in stressful situations? How can you improve your emotional intelligence to better connect with your team and stakeholders?

How can you encourage emotional intelligence and empathy within your organization? What programs or initiatives can you implement to support emotional well-being at all levels?

4. *Compassionate Leadership in Healthcare:*
How are you fostering a culture of compassionate care in your healthcare organization? What more can you do to ensure that both patients and healthcare workers feel supported and valued?

How can you better support healthcare workers who are dealing with stress and burnout? What steps can you take to create a more compassionate, resilient workforce?

Final Thoughts: Compassion as a Catalyst for Leadership

Compassionate leadership includes kindness, and yet it is about creating stronger, more connected, and more successful organizations. By leading with heart, you can build trust, foster innovation, and inspire your team to achieve greatness. Whether you're an entrepreneur, an executive, or a healthcare leader, compassion is a powerful tool that can drive both personal and organizational transformation.

In a world that often emphasizes results over relationships, compassionate leaders stand out. They understand that success is not measured solely by profits or performance, but by the positive impact they have on the people they lead. By embracing compassion as a core leadership principle, you can create a legacy that goes beyond the bottom line and leaves a lasting mark on your organization and the world.

Obiter Dictum:

In my years leading health systems, I have seen that leadership is more about connection than control. Compassion is an integral component to operational strategy. The organizations that endure are those that put people first: clinicians, staff, and patients alike. Dr. Paul Farmer and Dame Cicely Saunders were both driven by purpose, not profit. Their legacies remind us that healthcare is personal, and leadership must be as well. Whether we are building a culture, launching a program, or managing a crisis, we must lead with *empathy at scale*. It is not only how systems heal and prosper, but also how leaders leave something worth remembering.

Scenario:

Your organization faces burnout, emotional exhaustion, and disconnection.

What Would a Worthy Roman Imperator Do?

Lead like Dame Cicely Saunders or Yvon Chouinard with empathy and care. Compassion is the oil that keeps the machinery of achievement running.

While compassion often takes center stage, some of the most powerful forces remain unseen. Roman women influenced empires without fanfare. Their stories show us that influence will not always roar, often, it whispers through legacy.

"Silent influence often leaves the deepest marks."

–Roman maxim (attributed to the
historian Valerius Maximus)

CHAPTER X

Beyond the Marble: The Silent Might of Roman Matrons

Focus: The unseen often outlasts the visible. This chapter uncovers the impact of Roman women and the lessons they offer in subtle, strategic, and sustained influence.

L eadership is not always about a formal title or authority. It often unfolds through influence, wisdom, and resilience, especially when circumstances limit formal power. In ancient Rome, women were rarely in official positions of power, yet some wielded significant influence in both family and political spheres. This chapter explores how Roman women led by example, used strategic thinking to protect their families, and advanced their causes by building partnerships and adapting to social constraints. Their quiet but powerful leadership offers modern insights into influence without authority, resilience, and the art of persuasion.

Lessons Learned:

Leadership without a formal title can be just as impactful. Roman women leveraged relationships and social roles to guide decision-making within their households and, at times, in government.

Resilience and adaptability are crucial in navigating constraints. Roman women adapted to shifting dynamics and limited resources, influencing events from behind the scenes and orchestrating leadership from the wings of the political arena.

Leading through influence requires wisdom, subtlety, and trust. By building relationships and gaining the confidence of powerful men, Roman women left legacies that shaped the empire.

Case Studies in Roman Women's Leadership

I. Livia Drusilla: The Power Behind the Throne

Background: Livia Drusilla (58 BC–29 AD) was the wife of Emperor Augustus, and she exerted influence over Roman politics for decades. While officially she had no political power, she acted as a trusted advisor to Augustus and was highly respected in the Roman Senate.

Leadership Style: Livia embodied strategic influence. Known for her intelligence and poise, she guided Augustus' decisions and helped secure the imperial line. She cultivated relationships with key Senate members and demonstrated diplomacy, playing a subtle but essential role in establishing the stability of Augustus' reign.

Modern Takeaway: Livia's quiet authority shows that leaders can have an impact without a formal title, shaping decisions through trusted relationships and strategic alliances. Leaders today, especially those in advisory roles or collaborative environments, can benefit from her example by cultivating strong, influential relationships and leading through guidance.

II. Agrippina the Younger: Resilience and Ambition in a Restrictive Environment

Background: Agrippina the Younger (15–59 AD) was the mother of Emperor Nero and niece of Emperor Caligula. Known for her intelligence and determination, Agrippina navigated the treacherous world of Roman politics to secure her son's position on the throne.

Leadership Style: Agrippina was a master of political resilience. She skillfully maneuvered through the constraints placed on women, using her status and family connections to build alliances and negotiate power for her son. Though her methods were controversial, her adaptability and ambition ensured that her family remained influential in Roman politics.

Modern Takeaway: Agrippina's life highlights the power of resilience in hostile environments. Leaders today, particularly those facing structural obstacles, can learn from Agrippina's ability to adapt and influence from within, using available resources creatively and advocating for their causes with persistence.

III. Cornelia Africana: The Legacy of Maternal Leadership

Background: Cornelia Africana (c. 190–100 BC), mother of the Gracchi brothers, is celebrated for her wisdom and dedication to her family. As a widow, she raised her sons with a strong sense of duty to Rome, instilling in them ideals that influenced their later political reforms.

Leadership Style: Cornelia exemplified maternal leadership, shaping her sons' values and ambitions to serve Rome. Although not politically active herself, she was regarded as a role model of integrity and virtue, inspiring others through her example.

Modern Takeaway: Cornelia's legacy shows the impact of leading by example and cultivating strong values in those around us. Leaders can apply her lessons by focusing on mentoring and nurturing future leaders, emphasizing ethics, and fostering a sense of responsibility toward greater causes.

IV. Julia Domna: Scholar and Political Advisor

Background: Julia Domna (c. 160–217 AD) was the wife of Emperor Septimius Severus and mother of Emperor Caracalla. Known for her intellect and interest in philosophy, she gathered scholars, writers, and politicians around her, and acted as a key advisor to her husband.

Leadership Style: Julia demonstrated *intellectual leadership* and *strategic partnership.* By hosting salons and discussions, she influenced policy indirectly and created a network of scholars and thinkers who furthered the empire's intellectual pursuits.

Modern Takeaway: Julia's role underscores the value of intellectual influence and networking. Leaders who cultivate a network of informed advisors and engage in continuous learning, as Julia did, can drive meaningful change within their organizations.

Special Section for Healthcare Executives: Influence without Authority

In healthcare, leaders do not always have direct authority over every aspect of patient care, policy, or even their own organizations. Similar to the strategy of Roman women who led from behind the scenes, healthcare executives often influence outcomes by building coalitions, working across departments, and cultivating relationships with key stakeholders.

Practical Tips for Healthcare Leaders:

Build strong interdisciplinary relationships: Engage with professionals across departments to influence healthcare outcomes and ensure policies are patient-centered.

Advocate through trusted advisors: Like Livia Drusilla, build alliances with influential colleagues to further your organization's mission and objectives.

Lead by example: Demonstrate integrity, resilience, and empathy in your interactions, setting a standard of excellence for the organization.

Lessons from Women Leading Behind the Scenes

Practice subtle influence: Like Livia Drusilla, think of ways to influence decisions through advisory roles or partnerships. Identify key stakeholders in your organization and consider how you can build trust to make an impact.

Develop resilience under constraints: Inspired by Agrippina the Younger, list three challenges you currently face. For each, brainstorm a creative solution that uses available resources or relationships to overcome these obstacles.

Foster values in your organization: Like Cornelia Africana, work on instilling core values in your team or organization. Identify a value you'd like to emphasize and one action you can take this week to promote it among your colleagues or team.

Key Takeaways from Roman Women's Leadership

Roman women such as Livia Drusilla, Agrippina the Younger, Cornelia Africana, and Julia Domna were not just passive figures; they were strategists, advisors, and mentors. Though they led without formal authority, they created powerful legacies by navigating challenges, cultivating strong values, and influencing those around them effectively.

Influence without Authority: Leadership does not always come from a title; it can emerge through guidance, mentorship, and trust.

Adaptability and Resilience: Roman women adapted to complex and restrictive environments, a lesson in resilience for modern leaders.

Values and Legacy: By leading through influence and example, they left a lasting impact, proving that leadership can take many forms.

This chapter expands the leadership lessons to include nontraditional paths, showing that influence, resilience, and strategic partnerships are universal aspects of effective leadership, regardless of one's official title or position.

"Influence without Authority" can serve as a wise approach for any leader utilizing the example of key Roman women who often led behind the scenes, guiding decisions elegantly but effectively, allowing others to feel ownership of the outcomes.

Profile of Livia Drusilla— Leadership through Subtle Influence

Livia Drusilla: The Power Behind the Throne

Core Leadership Lesson: Influence without direct authority.

Insight: Livia Drusilla, wife of Augustus, mastered the art of subtle influence. Though she had no official title or political power, her role as Augustus' trusted advisor helped stabilize the empire during its early days. Through her intelligence, diplomacy, and strategic alliances, she became one of the most influential figures in Rome.

Modern Takeaway: Livia's approach highlights that true influence comes not from position but from trust, strategic relationships, and wise counsel. Leaders today can cultivate similar influence by building relationships and proving themselves as steady, thoughtful advisors.

Leading through Influence without Authority

Develop your "network of allies": Livia Drusilla cultivated strong relationships with members of the Senate and key political players, enabling her to advise Augustus effectively. Identify colleagues or mentors within your organization who share your goals and values. Connect with them regularly to exchange insights and support.

Identify where you can lead by example: Cornelia Africana shaped her sons' values and sense of duty by setting a personal standard of integrity and wisdom. Choose one value you'd like to reinforce in your organization. This week, look for an opportunity to demonstrate it through your actions, rather than directives.

Practice resilience through adaptability: Agrippina the Younger adjusted her strategies based on the ever-shifting political environment of Rome. Reflect on a current challenge you're facing. List two alternative approaches you could take to work around constraints, focusing on how you can influence outcomes indirectly if direct action isn't possible.

Reflection Questions

1. *How can you leverage influence without formal authority?*
   Reflect on ways to build relationships and foster trust that allows you to shape outcomes.

2. *Are you focusing on resilience and adaptability in your leadership approach?*
   Consider how you can adapt to limitations or challenges by using the resources at hand.

3. *How can you mentor future leaders like Cornelia Africana?*
   Identify one or two people you can actively mentor or guide, fostering values and skills that align with your organization's goals.

Obiter Dictum:

At one time I believed leadership needed to be bold and directive; however, I have humbly learned that the strongest leaders often work behind the scenes. Quiet influence is powerful. It builds trust without seeking attention.

In leadership, it often becomes inevitable that we focus on the loudest voice in the room, the one with the title, the microphone, the influence on paper. We are naturally pulled in that direction; nevertheless, in my years of leading organizations, especially in healthcare, I have seen that the people who really move us forward often do so without recognition. Their influence is built quietly through *trust, follow-through, and careful counsel.* Like Livia

Drusilla or Cornelia Africana, they shape culture, protect values, and guide outcomes through relationships and resilience.

As leaders, we must continue to recognize that not all leadership is positional, and our responsibility is to seek out, empower, and honor those who lead through character, not just hierarchy. True leaders make others better, even from behind the curtain. And sometimes, that is exactly where the best leadership happens.

Scenario:

You realize the quiet contributors—the "unsung heroes"—are your greatest asset.

What Would a Worthy Roman Imperator Do?

Honor them like Livia and Julia Domna: Support the strategic players behind the scenes. The invisible scaffolding that holds the empire aloft bears the greatest weight.

Leadership from the shadows still shaped the public arena. Now, we step directly into governance; where power is visible, debated, and shared. How did emperors and senators balance authority and advice? Rome shows the way.

"The noblest motive is the public good."

–Virgil

CHAPTER XI

Thrones and Forums: Balancing Governance and Influence

Focus: Leadership thrives when power is shared with wisdom. This chapter explores the tension and harmony between decisive authority and collaborative governance.

Nerva (96–98 CE) may not have had the long reign of Augustus or the legendary conquests of Trajan, but his leadership proved that even two short years can change history. Taking the throne after the assassination of Domitian, a tyrant who made both the Senate and Rome's people tremble, Nerva inherited an empire on the verge of collapse. His challenge? To restore trust and balance without alienating the Senate or the military. No pressure.

A Diplomatic Repair Job

Nerva's first move was a bold one: he vowed to never execute a senator, a clear departure from Domitian's reign of terror. He saw it as a very necessary and calculated step to rebuild the relationship between the emperor and the Senate. Nerva also adopted a more consultative style of governance, giving the Senate a voice in decisions. Think of it as Rome's version of collaborative leadership.

But it was not all smooth sailing. Nerva faced a significant challenge when the military, still loyal to Domitian, began to test his authority. In one infamous moment, the Praetorian Guard took Nerva hostage and demanded that he punish Domitian's assassins. Nerva, though humiliated, handled the crisis with grace, ultimately adopting Trajan, a beloved and capable general, as his heir. This move not only secured the loyalty of the military but also set a precedent for the peaceful transfer of power.

Small Reign, Big Impact

Despite his short reign, Nerva left a lasting legacy. His adoption of Trajan ensured Rome's stability for decades to come, and his reforms laid the groundwork for a more balanced government. Nerva's leadership can serve as a model for taking the necessary actions to make an organization successful and setting the stage for others to succeed.

Lessons for Modern Leaders

Collaborate to rebuild trust. Nerva's willingness to work with the Senate shows the power of collaboration, especially after a period of turmoil. Leaders today can use this approach to rebuild trust within teams or organizations.

Don't be afraid to share power. By adopting Trajan, Nerva proved that empowering others isn't a weakness, it is a strength. Modern leaders can follow his example by delegating authority and mentoring future leaders.

Handle crises with humility. Nerva's grace under pressure

during the Praetorian Guard rebellion reminds us that even when things go wrong, staying calm and strategic can lead to a positive outcome.

The Quiet Strategist

Nerva may not have statues or epic poems celebrating his reign, but his influence is felt in the stability he restored to Rome. He reminds us that leadership does not always have to be loud or flashy to make a difference.

The Roman governance system featured a unique balance of power between the emperors (Caesars) and the Senate. This interplay highlights the importance of balancing strong executive leadership with collaborative advisory input, a principle still vital in modern organizations. This chapter explores how Roman emperors leveraged the Senate's collective wisdom to make well-informed decisions, as well as the importance of balancing centralized authority with diverse perspectives. Leaders today can gain valuable insights into creating advisory structures that foster accountability, collaboration, and a culture of shared governance.

Lessons Learned:

Centralized Authority and Collaborative Counsel: Rome's Caesars often had final say, but successful emperors knew the value of collaboration with the Senate, using it as a source of diverse insights.

Balancing Authority with Accountability: Emperors who embraced collaboration with the Senate were more successful in earning the loyalty of the people, reinforcing that balanced power improves organizational trust and resilience.

Adapting Leadership to the Situation: Whether a leader adopts a "Caesar" or "Senator" approach depends on the situation. True leadership is about knowing when to make a decisive call and when to seek counsel.

Case Studies in Roman Governance

I. Augustus—Establishing Collaborative Leadership with the Senate

Background: Augustus, Rome's first emperor, knew that securing power meant more than exerting control; it required legitimacy. Augustus respected the Senate's advisory role and often deferred to it publicly, reinforcing a sense of shared governance that stabilized the early empire.

Leadership Style: Augustus exemplified *collaborative governance* by sharing credit with the Senate, which strengthened his position and the empire's stability. His approach helped unite the Senate and Roman citizens under a shared vision for a peaceful, prosperous empire.

Modern Takeaway: Augustus' respect for advisory input demonstrates that collaborative governance fosters loyalty and stability. Leaders can benefit by sharing credit with their teams and inviting diverse perspectives to strengthen decision-making.

II. Tiberius—The Cost of Isolating Authority

Background: Tiberius, Augustus' successor, preferred isolation and had a tense relationship with the Senate. Unlike Augustus, Tiberius distrusted the Senate and often made unilateral decisions without seeking Senate counsel, leading to growing discontent.

Leadership Style: Tiberius displayed a *centralized, isolated leadership* approach that alienated key advisors and weakened his influence. His reluctance to engage the Senate led to political instability, making his reign far less effective.

Modern Takeaway: Tiberius' isolation serves as a cautionary tale about the dangers of ignoring diverse perspectives. Leaders who avoid collaborative input risk making biased decisions and alienating their teams, weakening the organization over time.

III. Marcus Aurelius—Philosophical Balance Between Power and Counsel

Background: Marcus Aurelius was known for his philosophical approach to governance, balancing executive power with a deep respect for Senate input. He encouraged open debate within the Senate, creating an atmosphere where senators felt valued and empowered to speak honestly.

Leadership Style: Marcus Aurelius practiced *balanced governance* by incorporating his Senate counsel while also making thoughtful, decisive choices. His inclusive approach to leadership fostered a sense of unity, enabling Rome to withstand challenges during his reign.

Modern Takeaway: Marcus Aurelius shows that fostering open dialogue with advisors and weighing multiple perspectives strengthens leadership. His approach teaches today's leaders the value of balancing authority with input to build resilient organizations.

Special Section for Healthcare Executives: Collaborative Leadership in Complex Systems

Healthcare executives, like Roman Caesars, often hold centralized authority but work within complex systems where input from various departments is crucial. Just as Roman emperors relied on the Senate to understand diverse perspectives, healthcare leaders can benefit from advisory teams that represent multiple areas of expertise. Collaborative decision-making in healthcare can improve patient care, staff engagement, and operational efficiency.

Practical Tips for Healthcare Leaders

Establish advisory committees: Form committees that bring together voices from clinical, administrative, and operational roles to provide a well-rounded perspective on policies and procedures.

Encourage cross-departmental collaboration: Like Augustus with the Senate, embolden team members to share ideas and take ownership, fostering unity and shared responsibility for healthcare outcomes.

What Would a Worthy Roman Imperator Do?
Emulating Rome's Balanced Governance

Build your "Senate": Like Augustus, create a president's council, advisory group, or "mini-Senate" within your organization. Identify individuals who represent different areas of expertise and invite them to participate in regular strategy sessions.

Foster a culture of open debate: Marcus Aurelius encouraged senators to speak freely. To replicate this, consider holding open-forum meetings or regular check-ins where team members feel comfortable sharing insights and offering constructive criticism.

Know when to act as "Caesar" and when to listen like a "Senator": Situational leadership is key to success. When facing a high-stakes decision, assess whether it requires immediate action (a "Caesar" decision) or whether it would benefit from additional input (a "Senator" approach). Leaders who learn to adjust between these roles build stronger, more adaptable organizations.

Profile of Augustus—The Art of Collaborative Governance

Augustus: Rome's Master of Shared Leadership

Core Leadership Lesson: Balancing power with strategic collaboration.

Insight: As Rome's first emperor, Augustus established a cooperative governance model that preserved the Senate's influence, creating a stable foundation for his rule. This balance of power and counsel ensured long-term stability and set a precedent for future emperors.

Modern Takeaway: Augustus' collaborative approach highlights the power of balanced governance. By respecting the expertise and insights of advisory groups, modern leaders can create a unified organizational culture that encourages loyalty and shared purpose.

Key Takeaways from Rome's Governance Structure

The dynamic between Rome's emperors (Caesars) and senators offers timeless lessons in leadership. While the Caesars held ultimate authority, wise emperors understood the value of Senate counsel. This balance of power teaches leaders that true success comes from harmonizing authority with collaborative input.

Leadership Flexibility: Effective leaders know when to act decisively and when to seek advisory perspectives, balancing assertiveness with inclusivity.

Strengthening Loyalty through Unity: Just as Augustus gained support from the Senate, modern leaders who embrace collaboration strengthen trust and loyalty within their teams.

Building Resilient Governance Structures: Advisory groups are critical in today's complex environments. Leaders who implement advisory structures foster a resilient, accountable culture where ideas can flourish.

Reflection Questions

1. *How do you balance authority and collaboration in your leadership style?*
   Reflect on areas where you could seek more advisory input and where decisive action is required.

2. *Is there an advisory structure in place within your organization?*
   If not, consider creating one. If so, assess its effectiveness and how well it represents diverse perspectives.

3. *Are you fostering open dialogue?*
   Marcus Aurelius was a leader who encouraged open debate. Think of ways to create a consistent and productive environment for team members to share insights, feedback, and concerns.

Final Thoughts:

This chapter on "Caesars and Senators" explores governance through the lens of Roman authority and collaborative counsel, offering readers a model for balancing decisive leadership with advisory input. The examples from Roman history demonstrate that success often depends on a leader's ability to harness both centralized power and collective wisdom.

Obiter Dictum:

In boardrooms and hospital command centers, I have experienced what happens when authority is not balanced with humility. The best leaders I know do not hoard power; they invite perspective and still know when to decide.

The wisdom of Nerva, Augustus, and Marcus Aurelius exemplify that *true leadership is about orchestration.* In modern organizations, especially healthcare systems, the best outcomes are born from *shared governance,* not siloed command.

I have experienced firsthand that leaders who *build councils, empower others, and welcome input* foster cultures of trust, agility, and sustained excellence. It sometimes takes strength to be decisive, but as a true leader, it takes even greater strength to demonstrate the wisdom of *when to act boldly and when to listen deeply.*

Scenario:

An urgent decision splits your advisors. Command versus consensus—who wins?

What Would a Worthy Roman Imperator Do?

Be like Augustus in his prime: Balance authority with wisdom. Listen deeply and decide firmly. True power truly blends counsel and command.

Governance is dialogue. But dialogue must eventually give way to design. In the next chapter, we explore how strategic infrastructure, both literal and organizational, becomes the foundation of enduring greatness.

*"Let the foundations be deep and the stones set with
care—so the empire may outlive the builder."*

–paraphrased from Vitruvius' architectural principles

CHAPTER XII

The Infrastructure of Greatness: Aqueducts, Roads, and Strategic Systems

*Focus: Greatness is engineered. This chapter
reveals how sustainable leadership is constructed
through systems thinking and legacy design.*

Constantine the Great (272–337 AD) reinvented the empire he ruled. Rising to power during a turbulent era, Constantine brought sweeping change to the Roman world. Known as the first Christian emperor, he instituted religious reforms and went on to found *Constantinople*, a city designed to become the empire's new cultural and political heart. Constantine's reign is the story of a leader who balanced bold innovation with long-term vision.

The Birth of Constantinople

Rome had been the center of power for centuries, but Constantine saw its vulnerabilities: the city was old, geographically exposed, and politically fractured. So, what did Emperor Constantine determine was the best way forward? He constructed a *new* Rome. In 324 AD, he transformed the Greek city of Byzantium into Constantinople, a dazzling metropolis strategically located between Europe and Asia. Constantinople became the hub of trade, culture, and politics, sustaining the empire for another thousand years.

Modern leaders can take inspiration from this by recognizing when a shift is needed to address future challenges. Sometimes, creating a "new Rome" is the only way forward.

A Religious Revolution

Constantine's conversion to Christianity impacted his personal life and changed history. In 313 AD, he issued the *Edict of Milan*, granting religious tolerance throughout the empire. By aligning himself with Christianity, Constantine unified a growing movement, giving Rome a new cultural identity that would shape Western civilization.

This bold decision demonstrates how leaders can use cultural shifts to unite their organizations. Constantine adopted Christianity and wove it into the very fabric of the empire, creating an impactful and lasting legacy. You can too.

Military and Administrative Reforms

Constantine was also a military innovator. He reorganized the army to strengthen borders and ensure the empire could withstand external threats. Internally, he restructured the bureaucracy, creating a more centralized and efficient government.

Leadership Lesson: Constantine's reign is a Master Class in balancing bold innovation with practical governance. Modern leaders can emulate his vision by identifying long-term opportunities while ensuring their organizations are resilient in the face of change.

Legacy of a Visionary

Constantine's impact is hard to overstate. From the creation of Constantinople to the rise of Christianity, his leadership reshaped Rome and the world. If you're facing a challenge that seems insurmountable, ask yourself: *What bold vision could I pursue that would redefine my organization for the future?*

The Roman Empire's groundbreaking infrastructure innovations on everything from roads, aqueducts, concrete, and even legal systems, enabled the entire empire to thrive and expand. These innovations were not merely functional; they created lasting stability and connected the empire in ways that allowed for efficient governance and economic growth. This chapter examines these Roman breakthroughs as a model for modern leaders, emphasizing the importance of creating foundational systems that enhance resilience, adaptability, and connectivity. By investing in strong, sustainable systems, today's leaders can build organizations capable of thriving in an ever-changing world.

Lessons Learned:

Invest in Resilient Infrastructure: Just as Romans built enduring aqueducts and roads, modern leaders must create robust structures (whether digital or operational) that support long-term stability and growth.

Prioritize Connectivity and Accessibility: Roman roads connected people and markets across the empire, fostering economic and social cohesion. Leaders today should focus on connectivity within their organizations (including those remote) to drive unity and facilitate efficient communication.

Commit to Sustainability: Roman innovations were designed to last, teaching modern leaders the value of systems and processes that withstand the test of time.

Case Studies in Roman Innovations

I. The Aqueducts—Providing Resources to Fuel Growth

Background: Rome's aqueducts were engineering marvels, bringing water from distant sources into urban centers, supplying public baths, fountains, and private homes. This steady water supply supported urban expansion, public health, and economic prosperity.

Leadership Lesson: The aqueducts showcase *resource-focused governance.* Rome prioritized essential resources that enabled its cities to thrive. By investing in infrastructure that improved public welfare, Roman leaders set the stage for sustainable growth.

Modern Takeaway: Leaders today can follow this example by investing in resources essential to team productivity and well-being, such as technology, training, and wellness programs.

II. Roman Roads—Connectivity for Efficient Governance

Background: Roman roads stretched over 250,000 miles, facilitating trade, communication, and military movement. This network connected the empire's farthest reaches, allowing for efficient governance and rapid response to regional issues.

Leadership Lesson: Roman roads exemplify the importance of *connectivity and accessibility.* Leaders understood that a connected empire was a resilient one, able to respond to crises and seize opportunities.

Modern Takeaway: Today's leaders can emulate this by creating "road networks" of communication within their organizations. Encouraging transparency and accessible information flow fosters unity and enables swift decision-making across departments.

III. Concrete—Building Durable Foundations

Background: Roman concrete, known for its durability and resilience, enabled the construction of iconic structures such as the Pantheon and the Colosseum. Unlike modern concrete, Roman concrete became stronger over time, supporting structures that still remain today.

Leadership Lesson: The durability of Roman concrete symbolizes *building strong foundations* that endure. Rome's investment in resilient materials allowed it to create infrastructure that lasted centuries, a testament to its long-term planning.

Modern Takeaway: Leaders today should invest in processes and systems that strengthen over time, focusing on sustainable growth rather than short-term gains. Such as developing training programs, robust operational systems, or ethical guidelines that reinforce organizational resilience.

IV. Roman Law—Establishing Standards for Governance

Background: Roman law provided a unified legal framework across the empire, setting precedents that influenced Western legal systems for centuries. It established justice, fairness, and order, contributing to a stable society.

Leadership Lesson: Roman law represents the value of *consistent governance standards.* By implementing fair and uniform policies, Rome maintained order and public trust.

Modern Takeaway: Today's leaders can establish clear, consistent standards in organizational policies, fostering a culture of fairness and trust. Whether through transparent HR practices or ethical guidelines, standardized systems contribute to a stable work environment.

Special Section for Healthcare Executives: Building Sustainable Systems

In healthcare, resilient and sustainable systems are essential for delivering consistent patient care. Just as Roman aqueducts ensured access to vital resources, modern healthcare leaders must invest in systems that support both staff and patient well-being. Building strong foundations in healthcare operations, such as reliable supply chains, digital connectivity, and clear communication frameworks, ensures quality care and organizational stability.

Practical Tips for Healthcare Leaders:

Invest in essential resources: Ensure your team has the necessary tools, technology, and support systems to deliver high-quality care.

Create "roadways" for efficient communication: Facilitate connectivity across departments to ensure smooth, collaborative care delivery and quick response times.

Standardize care practices: Like Roman law, establish consistent care standards that uphold quality, fairness, and trust within your organization.

What Would Rome Do? Building Lasting Systems for Modern Organizations

Identify your "aqueduct": Like Roman aqueducts, every organization has essential resources that fuel its productivity and growth. Pinpoint a critical resource, such as technology, knowledge-sharing systems, or employee wellness, and strategize how to ensure its reliable availability and impact.

Establish your "road network": Connectivity was key to Rome's success. Assess your organization's communication structure. Consider setting up regular cross-departmental meetings, project management systems, or information-sharing platforms to keep your team unified and informed.

Build with resilience in mind: Just as Roman concrete strengthened with time, create processes or policies that become increasingly more effective. For example, implement continuous learning programs for employees or create long-term partnerships that grow and strengthen your organization's network.

Profile of Roman Roads—Connecting the Empire for Stability and Growth

Roman Roads: The First Superhighway

Core Leadership Lesson: Prioritize connectivity and accessible communication.

Insight: Roman roads stretched across the empire, allowing leaders to govern distant regions effectively and respond swiftly to issues. By building infrastructure that facilitated movement and communication, Rome fostered unity and cohesion.

Modern Takeaway: Leaders today can apply this principle by creating strong communication channels within their organizations. A connected organization is better equipped to respond to challenges, seize opportunities, and maintain alignment.

Key Takeaways from Roman Innovations

Roman innovations in infrastructure and governance serve as models for building resilient, adaptable organizations. From aqueducts to concrete, these innovations demonstrate the value of investing in systems that prioritize long-term impact over short-term gains. For today's leaders, Rome's breakthroughs offer practical lessons in developing stable, sustainable structures that support growth and enable efficient governance.

Resilient Infrastructure: Strong, reliable foundations ensure an organization can adapt to changing circumstances without compromising stability.

Connectivity and Unity: Like Roman roads, accessible communication channels create unity and empower an organization to move as one.

Standards of Governance: Consistent policies and guidelines, modeled after Roman law, foster trust, stability, and shared values across an organization.

Reflection Questions

1. *Are you investing in foundational resources for your team?*

   Consider areas where resource investment could improve performance or morale.

2. *How connected is your organization?*

   Assess your organization's communication channels. Could information flow be improved to enhance collaboration and speed up decision-making?

3. *What systems are in place to ensure long-term resilience?*

   Reflect on existing policies or practices that reinforce stability and identify areas for improvement.

Final Thoughts:

This chapter on *Roman Innovations to Modern Breakthroughs* provides a valuable perspective on building long-lasting, resilient systems that are essential for sustainable governance and organizational stability. The examples of Roman infrastructure offer actionable insights for modern leaders, reinforcing the importance of investing in structures that support growth, connectivity, and resilience over time.

Obiter Dictum:

When redesigning our care systems, we made sure our purpose drove the technological decision-making. The infrastructure behind the scenes either enables greatness or blocks it. Make the correct decision in the beginning, and everything else flows.

Constantine was a great leader. Like many great leaders, he wisely responded to the present while he built for the future. His bold decision to found a new capital, embrace a rising faith, and centralize systems reveals a timeless leadership truth: *when the old architecture no longer serves, it is time to redesign the foundation.*

I have often shared with teams that the focus and discipline behind establishing infrastructure, whether it is cultural, operational, or technological, is not glamorous; nevertheless, it is the invisible framework that enables everything else to thrive. Like aqueducts, great systems do not call attention to themselves. They just work well, quietly enabling excellence every day.

Today's healthcare and organizational leaders must adopt this mindset. We are not here to chase applause, but to engineer systems of strength and resilience. Think beyond the quarter. Build what lasts.

Scenario:

You are under pressure to show quick wins, but the system needs major foundational reform.

What Would a Worthy Roman Imperator Do?

Think like the aqueduct builders. Invest in systems invisible today but vital tomorrow. Greatness is engineered for endurance, not applause.

Bricks and aqueducts may endure, but what of the mind? Roman brilliance wasn't only in stone, but in thought. Our journey now turns to the discipline of reflection and the quiet strength of cultivated wisdom.

"No man is truly great who is great only in his lifetime"

— Seneca

CHAPTER XIII

The Cultivated Mind: Lifelong Learning, Intellectual Discipline, and the Roman Art of Reflection

Focus: Wisdom, like Rome, is built over time. This chapter examines how intellectual curiosity and philosophical reflection, elevate decision-making, develop wisdom, and strengthen as well as anchor enduring leadership.

Rome conquered the world with its armies. But it ruled the world with its ideas. The Romans expanded their borders, and they expanded their minds.

From the Stoic solitude of Marcus Aurelius to the cutting observations of Seneca, Rome was the utmost military empire and an ultimate *civilization of thought.* Its greatest leaders were skilled in war, politics, and infrastructure, and they were also students of philosophy, seekers of wisdom, and lifelong learners.

They understood what many modern leaders forget: The *cultivated mind* is a requirement, not a luxury. It is a tool of survival.

In this chapter, we explore how Roman leaders pursued *intellectual growth,* how their embrace of philosophy shaped policy and power, and why today's leaders must become *strategic learners* in order to thrive in a world that never stops changing.

From military commanders to emperors, many of Rome's most influential leaders were men of extreme action as well as intellectual men of ideas. They read, they wrote, they questioned. They believed that a leader's external command was only as strong as their internal clarity.

To rule others well, you had to first rule yourself. Proper self-rule began with study.

In this chapter, we shift from building empires of roads and governance to exploring the empire of the mind: the inner terrain that determines whether a leader becomes resilient or rigid, wise or reactive, relevant or forgotten.

The Roman Obsession with Philosophy

For the Romans, philosophy was an academic subject that progressed as a daily discipline and matured as a lifetime view of how to see and behave in the world.

They turned to Stoicism, Epicureanism, and Platonism not as abstract thought experiments, but as practical tools for leadership and life.

Marcus Aurelius, the philosopher-emperor, penned his *Meditations* while managing plagues and wars, using reflection as armor and foundation.

Seneca, advisor to Nero, taught that clarity came from eliminating distractions and confronting your weaknesses.

Cicero, master orator and statesman, wielded philosophy as both shield and sword, using reasoned argument to preserve the republic.

To these men, a well-governed city was impossible without a well-governed soul.

Their writings remain timeless because their principles were never theoretical.

They lived their philosophies through crises, in courtrooms, and in command tents.

Roman leadership was not a performance. It was a way of life.

It was a philosophy in motion. A foundation for living.

Modern Leadership and the Lost Art of Reflections

Today's world often rewards speed over depth, reaction over reflection.

Too often, leaders neglect this inner work. They build dashboards, not philosophies. They chase influence but ignore introspection. However, in the modern arena, whether it's medicine, tech, business, or public service, there is a demand for continued awareness, followed by the demands of appropriate action.

The most effective modern leaders, those who build influence that lasts, rediscover what Rome always knew: wisdom is the highest form of strategy. It is a matter of gathering data and filtering it through principles. They operate with a great sense of urgency and yet still pause to consider all the ramifications. The successful are determined to maintain a continual consumption of knowledge for a purpose; to cultivate perspective and then take action.

The Philosopher-Emperor: Marcus Aurelius

Let's begin with the man who never wanted to be emperor: Marcus Aurelius.

He was more philosopher than politician, more writer than warrior. And yet, he led Rome through plague, war, and unrest.

It was not leadership with fiery speeches, but with *quiet discipline* and a mind sharpened by study.

He did not benefit from a social media team.

He had a notebook.

Marcus didn't write for others.

He wrote for himself.

His daily discipline, to think through and reinforce what mattered.

Each morning, he would reflect before the day began. He was reminding himself of his values, his duties, his weaknesses, and his purpose. His words were often harsh, blunt, and humble. He criticized his own ego. He examined his fatigue. He told himself not to be bitter, even when betrayed.

He reminded himself that he was mortal.

That his temper needed work.

That people would disappoint him.

That he still had work to do.

He was writing forward.

He was writing accountability.

His reflections were his disciplined leadership gymnasium. The training of the mind like a Roman soldier trained his body and sword arm.

The result is what we now know as *Meditations.* It was never intended for anyone else's eyes. It was his private journal, filled with reflections, reminders, and self-corrections. It was his mirror and his map. And it shaped not only his leadership, but the legacy of an empire.

His example teaches us something vital:

The leader who reflects is the leader who can focus and refine.

Why Curiosity is a Leadership Skill

In modern leadership, we tend to reward decisiveness, speed, and confidence. But the Romans, and the best leaders today, recognized that sustainable leadership is not only knowing what to do, it is also about asking *why*, and *what comes next.*

Hadrian traveled widely throughout the empire as a statement of sovereignty, stability, and to gain a deeper understanding of the vast empire's people and their needs.

Cicero used rhetoric as a strength to persuade and convince; moreover, he also used to inquire and evolve.

Julius Caesar was a student of military tactics, and yet he also studied history, philosophy, and even astronomy, believing that the broader his learning, the sharper his insight.

Curiosity was not pursued for transient purposes or as a hobby.

It was a form of power and growth.

What they all have in common:

They saw learning as leadership. A never-ending focus and discipline.

What Learning Looks Like in Modern Empire Builders

Let's look at the modern leaders who lead with their minds.

Satya Nadella—Rewriting the Code of Curiosity

"Don't be a know-it-all. Be a learn-it-all." –Satya Nadella

When Satya Nadella took over as CEO of Microsoft in 2014, the tech giant was slowly calcifying. Once the dominant force in software, Microsoft had grown comfortable. Its internal culture had become defensive. Silos separated teams. Collaboration was minimal. Innovation felt forced. The company was still powerful, but it had lost its spark and recognized the deficit.

In the Roman Empire, this would have been a dangerous moment. A turning point between continued dominance and inevitable decline. Nadella understood this instinctively. But instead of marching in with top-down decrees or grand restructuring plans, he brought something unexpected to the leadership table: *humility and curiosity*.

One of his first moves? He recommended his executive team read *Mindset* by Carol Dweck. Surprisingly, the book did not focus on business strategy or even cloud computing, it was a book about how people learn. Nadella saw that the deepest issue at Microsoft was not its suffering from any type of technical or pure competitive deficit. It was cultural. It was fear of failure. A fixed mindset. A slow creep toward stagnation.

So he began rebuilding from the inside out.

At company town halls, he shifted the conversation from "What do we know?" to "What are we learning?" He praised experiments that failed but taught something. He listened more than he spoke. Engineers were encouraged to explore other teams' projects. Customers were invited into product design discussions. Instead of defending turf, Microsoft started *cultivating curiosity.*

He called this mindset shift the difference between a "know-it-all" and a "learn-it-all."

That single idea became the cornerstone of Microsoft's transformation. Under Nadella, the company grew from a lumbering tech titan to a revitalized leader in cloud computing, AI, and enterprise services. Its stock tripled. Its employees began to believe again. Its customers noticed the difference.

Nadella talked about curiosity and lived it. His personal leadership journal included reflections from his reading, questions he was struggling with, and big ideas he didn't yet know how to solve. He used writing as a way to think more clearly.

The daily discipline of written reflections, a distinctly Roman habit.

Like Hadrian traveling the provinces of Rome to understand the empire's edges, Nadella traveled Microsoft's internal terrain, as a journey to envision and discern, not command.

He was not trying to control the future. He was trying to expand his comprehension and *learn his way into it.*

Roman Parallel: Emperor Hadrian

Hadrian inherited an empire from Trajan that could be argued had overextended beyond its logistical limits and was unable to accommodate the empire's necessary resources. Instead of building outward, he paused expansion and turned inward. He traveled extensively. It was not for pageantry, but to observe, to ask questions, and to understand the lived experience of his people. His retrenchment was pragmatic and necessary for the empire's stability. Nadella followed a similar arc: slow down, consolidate, listen, and then evolve. Influence built on curiosity.

Empire of Influence Takeaway:

Nadella proved that curiosity is a form of strategic intelligence.

In fact, sometimes a business doesn't need a new product or service, it needs a new question. A depth of curiosity to be explored.

Dr. Atul Gawande—The Reflective Scalpel

"Better is possible. It does not take genius. It takes diligence. It takes moral clarity. It takes ingenuity. And above all, it takes a willingness to try." –Atul Gawande

Long before he became a global voice on systems reform and mortality, Dr. Atul Gawande stood in a hospital operating room, quietly studying the checklist taped to the wall.

It was simple. It listed steps. It didn't look revolutionary. And yet, it changed everything.

At the time, Gawande was a surgeon and a writer. But more than anything, he was a *student of failure.* He wanted to understand why, despite medical advancements, preventable errors continued to occur; why systems designed to save lives were often the very things that endangered them.

He began to notice something that few people in healthcare wanted to admit:

Complexity was not the enemy; complacency was the true issue.

Doctors assumed they'd remember the basics. Nurses assumed systems would catch errors. But no one paused long enough to ask, "What if we're wrong?"

That single question became Gawande's signature. He performed surgeries and interrogated the structures that supported the process. He challenged the systems, not relying on trust alone. As a physician, his writings were not only directed at other physicians, but also at the entire healthcare industry and beyond. He wrote to *change the way people think.*

In the *Checklist Manifesto,* Gawande argued that success in complex fields did not come from brilliance. It came from humility. From structure. From having people brave enough to say: "Let's slow down and do it right."

He traced how pilots use checklists to prevent crashes, how architects plan for disaster, how even seasoned chefs walk through the basics before every shift. This is not because they are incompetent, or forgetful, but because they were *disciplined.* In medicine, he applied the same thinking. Hospitals that adopted checklists saw dramatic drops in complications and mortality rates.

But Gawande did not stop at logistics. His next book, *Being Mortal*, confronted the *philosophical and emotional* blind spots of modern medicine. Why do we avoid conversations about death? Why do we treat longevity as success when dignity might matter more? What does it mean to care, not just treat?

These were not technical questions. They were *leadership questions*. And Gawande used them to provoke change in hospitals, policy rooms, and dining tables across the world.

Through it all, he led not as a physician or by title, but by thought. His influence came from his willingness to *observe, question, and write.*

Like Seneca in Nero's court, Gawande's power came not as a result of his position, but from his principles.

His influence extended to global health initiatives, pandemic preparedness, and even his appointment as Assistant Administrator for Global Health at USAID. Yet through each role, he stayed grounded in the same habit: *reflective inquiry.*

Where others rushed to act, he paused to learn.

Where others chased new procedures, he asked, "What is the human cost?"

Where others assumed success, he asked, "Is this truly better?"

Roman Parallel: Seneca

Seneca, like Gawande, occupied a complex position of influence. He advised power. He navigated politics. But his most lasting legacy wasn't his proximity to the emperor—it was his writings on life, death, clarity, and control. Seneca taught that wisdom requires reflection, and that courage means facing uncomfortable truths.

Gawande, too, has made his name by doing what others

would not: confronting complexity with clarity and calm. In a profession trained to avoid vulnerability, he modeled it. An approach of openness, and the desire to always improve.

Empire of Influence Takeaway:

Leadership requires outcomes but not results alone. It is about asking *why* we do what we do. Dr. Atul Gawande reminds us that a steady hand is most powerful when guided by a thoughtful mind.

Dr. Fei-Fei Li—Architect of Ethical Intelligence

"Technology doesn't just change the world—it reveals who we are."
–Fei-Fei Li

In 2007, Dr. Fei-Fei Li helped launch one of the most influential datasets in artificial intelligence history: ImageNet. It was a massive visual database, painstakingly built, designed to help machines see and interpret the world, and it would fuel some of the most rapid advances in computer vision and AI over the next decade.

But while others celebrated the speed of progress, Fei-Fei Li began asking deeper questions.

What is AI really learning, and from whom?

Are we teaching it fairness? Bias? Ethics?

Who is shaping the future of intelligence, and who is being left out?

Fei-Fei Li does not only serve as a computer scientist. She's also a philosopher-engineer. A modern Roman of the mind. She holds a PhD in electrical engineering from Caltech, has taught at Princeton and Stanford, led AI development at Google Cloud, and helped set policy at the national level. In fact, at every stage, her influence originates from her credentials as well as from her established *ethical clarity*.

In her keynote speeches and articles, she consistently returns to one theme:

"AI is not only designed code. It is about *character.*"

She warned early on that AI systems, if trained on biased data, would reflect and even amplify society's prejudices. Facial recognition programs, for example, often performed poorly on darker-skinned individuals. It was not because of malice, but because the data used to train them was flawed and incomplete. These are human oversights, not technical errors.

Rather than ignore this, Fei-Fei Li made it her mission to humanize artificial intelligence.

She co-founded *AI4ALL*, a non-profit aimed at increasing diversity and inclusion in the field of AI. Its goal is to equip young women, students of color, and other underrepresented groups with the skills and the voice to help shape the future of technology.

She believes that *who builds AI is as important as what it can do.*

When asked to comment on AI's potential military applications during her time at Google, she didn't avoid controversy. She spoke out. She urged transparency. She challenged her colleagues and herself to *consider the moral weight* of their creations. She was attempting to influence the future. Her stated desire has been to shape it with purpose.

Just as Marcus Aurelius led through moral restraint during military campaigns, Fei-Fei Li believes leadership in innovation must be guided by responsibility as much as vision.

What sets her apart is her advanced ability to think technically while also maintaining an exceptional *philosophical* approach and teaching others to do the same.

She tells her students to take courses outside of engineering: in literature, history, and ethics. She insists that machines may be learning fast, but *humans must learn faster about ourselves.*

Roman Parallel: Marcus Aurelius

Marcus Aurelius, like Fei-Fei Li, lived in an age of enormous power. He chose to meet it with restraint, humility and rigorous self-examination. He led armies, managed crises and governed an empire; furthermore, he was also a man of notebooks, a student of philosophy, and a guardian of values. Marcus Aurelius knew how to wield authority, but he was also visibly aware of the immense responsibility that came with that power and strove to navigate it appropriately and fairly.

Fei-Fei Li embodies that same duality. She commands one of the most powerful forces in our world, AI; yet speaks with the voice of a philosopher. Her desire to shape code is consistent with her endeavor to influence the conscience.

Empire of Influence Takeaway:

Fei-Fei Li shows us that true innovation requires reflection.

The future is an adventure we must appropriately build, and it is also something we must steward.

Today's leaders often neglect this inner work. They often demand metric performance but ignore the philosophies supporting a positive core. They chase influence but ignore the necessary introspection.

Whether it is medicine, tech, business, or public service, our modern arena urgently requires more than action.

It demands a depth of awareness.

Marcus Aurelius and the Morning Journal

"When you arise in the morning, think of what a privilege it is to be alive—to think, to enjoy, to love ..." **Marcus Aurelius**

I think it is worth repeating ...

Marcus didn't write for others.

He wrote for himself.

It wasn't his military might that made Marcus Aurelius remarkable. It was his extraordinary self-discipline.

Each day, he wrote. Not to impress. Not to publish.

He wrote to *clarify and remember what mattered.*

Scenario 1:

You're leading a high-performing team, but you sense disconnection and drift. You're constantly reacting, barely thinking. Everyone expects you to have the answers.

What Would a Worthy Roman Imperator Do?

Marcus would pause and write.

Seneca would question the assumption.

Cicero would argue the opposite viewpoint.

Hadrian would take a walk through the empire to see what he was missing.

Rome's immense strength came from its legions and from its thinkers. So take the time to think. It is not an assignment for later. It is a requirement, now.

Scenario 2:

Your team is looking to you for direction, but the landscape keeps changing. The old playbooks don't work. You're expected to know the answers, but you're not even sure whether you are asking all the right questions.

What Would a Worthy Roman Imperator Do?

Pause to study the moment.

Journal the challenge. Not the answers, just the thoughts.

Seek counsel from your "senate." Inquire with the trusted minds and advisors around you.

Ask better questions. That is where the breakthrough begins.

Lessons for Modern Leaders:

Stillness is a strategy. Great decisions are born in quiet, not chaos.

Curiosity is more important than certainty. Certainty calcifies. Curiosity creates.

Reflective leaders evolve. When you write, think, or discuss ideas, you clarify your mission.

Learning builds humility. It's harder to become arrogant when you are always a student.

Special Section for Healthcare Executives

Healthcare demands constant learning, from regulations to innovations. From systems thinking to cultural empathy. But how often do we institutionalize reflection?

Are your clinical leaders journaling after difficult cases?

Do your department heads reflect on their decision-making blind spots?

Are you giving space for intellectual recovery, or just procedural compliance?

What if your organization became a "learning empire," not just an "operating machine"? Encouraging reflective practice and philosophical questions could reduce burnout, improve outcomes, and reignite purpose across your leadership team.

Reflection Questions

1. *What personal routine helps you stay mentally clear and grounded?*

2. *Where do you go (physically or mentally) when you need to think deeply?*

3. *What is the last strategic decision where you changed your mind, and what triggered the shift?*

4. *What do you wish your younger leadership self had understood about learning?*

Final Thoughts

The best empires were built by hands, but they were guided by minds. The cultivated leader is a prepared leader. One who reads before acting, reflects before reacting, and builds not just for profit. A leader who also builds for posterity. In a world full of noise, the leader who dares to be a student…builds the longest legacy.

Obiter Dictum:

I still read, study, and reflect. I maintain these disciplines not because I have to, but because it keeps my perspective as a leader open and aware. The leaders I admire most never stop learning. They are experts, and yet they always remain students of the world around them.

Leadership is about guiding others, but it is also about *knowing oneself* well enough to lead with integrity, purpose, and wisdom. What has become apparent to me over the decades is that the *most resilient leaders are both doers and they are thinkers.*

This chapter brought to mind many moments when writing in my own journal gave me clarity and the peace I needed before stepping into a challenging meeting or making a hard call. We often overvalue the visible performance of leadership and undervalue the invisible preparation. But, like Marcus Aurelius, our private reflection fuels our public actions.

In healthcare especially, where the demands are high and the stakes even higher, creating daily time for reflective practice is not an indulgence. I submit it is the requirement of an *essential internal infrastructure for better outcomes. What you build within will ultimately shape what you build beyond.*

Scenario:

You are praised for results and yet personally stagnating, uninspired, and inwardly drained.

What Would a Worthy Roman Imperator Do?

Reflect like Marcus Aurelius. Study. Write. Think. The empire of the mind needs daily purposeful tending to match the impactful empire of action.

Reflection leads to intention and intention defines legacy. What will you build that endures beyond you? Like Rome, your leadership can span centuries if its foundations are clear, purposeful, and virtuous.

*"He lives most who is least afraid of death
and who can leave a legacy undying."*

— Seneca

CHAPTER XIV

Legacy in Motion

Focus: How to Build Influence That Lasts Beyond You

T hroughout this book, we've explored the multifaceted roles of leadership, from cultivating humility and fostering collaboration to driving innovation and managing crises. As today's entrepreneurs and executives, you face a world that is more connected, complex, and volatile than ever before. Whether you are navigating a startup through rapid growth, leading a corporation through economic uncertainty, or steering a healthcare organization through uncharted waters, the lessons you've learned here can guide you toward *building a leadership legacy that lasts.*

In this final chapter, we'll draw the threads together. You'll reflect on what it means to be a transformational leader in today's environment, where ethical decision-making, emotional intelligence, resilience, and vision are essential for success. We'll explore how you can apply the lessons from this book to create a *leadership blueprint* that not only drives results but also leaves a lasting impact on your organization, industry, and society.

The Evolution of Leadership: From Command to Collaboration

Leadership has evolved dramatically over the past few decades. In the early days of industrialization, leadership was about command and control, directing workers to produce more, faster, and cheaper. As organizations became more complex, leadership shifted toward management, where leaders focused on optimizing processes and achieving efficiency. Today, leadership is about something deeper: *influence, emotional intelligence, vision, and the ability to inspire others to achieve shared goals.*

In this book, we've seen the evolution of leadership through historical examples, case studies, and modern practices. Leaders like Marcus Aurelius, Walt Disney, Indra Nooyi, and Satya Nadella all demonstrated different facets of leadership that reflect today's demands: resilience, creativity, compassion, and ethical decision-making.

Now, as you reflect on your own leadership journey, it's time to ask yourself: *What kind of leader do you want to be?* Are you building a legacy that will endure beyond your tenure? Are you leading with authenticity and courage? The future of leadership demands a blend of traditional strengths, such as decisiveness and strategic thinking, with new competencies, such as empathy, adaptability, and collaboration.

Key Question: How has your leadership style evolved to meet the needs of today's world, and how can you continue to grow as a leader?

Case Study I: Elon Musk—Visionary Leadership for the Future

Whether you love him or loathe him, Elon Musk is a modern-day example of visionary leadership. Musk's companies: Tesla, SpaceX,

Neuralink, X, xAI, OpenAI, and The Boring Company are true manifestations of a future he boldly envisions. Musk's leadership style is adventurous, daring, and disruptive. He does not shy away from taking risks, often betting the future of his companies on technologies that do not yet exist. His vision of a world powered by sustainable energy, interplanetary travel, and brain-computer interfaces is ambitious, and his leadership reflects that audacity.

But Musk's leadership isn't without flaws. He's known for being a demanding leader, sometimes pushing his teams to the brink of burnout. While his vision drives incredible innovation, his relentless pace can lead to friction within his organizations. The lesson here is twofold: *visionary leadership can change the world*, but it must be balanced with compassion, empathy, and respect for the well-being of your team.

Empire of Influence Takeaway:

Vision without execution is hallucination. Musk's success stems from his ability to turn bold ideas into reality, but it requires a relentless focus on execution.

As a leader, you must *balance your vision with the ability to inspire and motivate your team* without pushing them too far. Are you supporting your team in realizing the vision, or are you burning them out in the pursuit of success?

Musk's leadership shows that while bold visionaries can lead the future, their legacy is only as strong as the teams they build and support.

Legacy Leadership: What Will You Leave Behind?

A central theme of this book has been the idea of *legacy leadership*. It is the real-life concept that leadership requires determined and consistent achievement today, combined with what you leave behind for others tomorrow. Legacy leaders understand that their influence extends far beyond their immediate impact. They focus on building systems, cultures, and organizations that can thrive in their absence.

One of the most profound examples of legacy leadership comes from Walt Disney. Disney's vision of a world of imagination and creativity wasn't limited to his lifetime. He built Disneyland and, later, Walt Disney World, as places where his vision could continue to flourish long after he was gone. His company has evolved, but the core values he instilled of innovation, creativity, and storytelling continue to guide the organization today.

As an entrepreneur or executive, your legacy is being built every day. It is not merely the products you launch or even the deals you close; it is the people you mentor, the culture you create, and the systems you put in place that will define your leadership legacy long after your tenure.

Key Question: What kind of legacy are you building? How will your leadership continue to influence your organization and industry after you've left?

Case Study II: Muhammad Yunus—Legacy of Empowerment through Innovation

When Muhammad Yunus looked at poverty, he didn't see a permanent social condition, he saw a failure of imagination. Where others viewed charity as the answer, he envisioned *empowerment.* And where traditional financial institutions saw poor people as too risky to invest in, Yunus saw an untapped source of energy, innovation, and growth. In doing so, he not only changed banking, but he also *rewrote the rules of economic systems* worldwide. Like the great Roman innovators who built aqueducts and roads not for prestige but for public utility, Yunus created structures that opened the floodgates of opportunity to millions.

The Birth of an Idea: Microfinance and the Grameen Bank

The story began in 1976 in Bangladesh. Yunus, an economics professor freshly returned from studies in the United States, found himself disillusioned with abstract theories while real people around him starved. One day, he lent $27 out of his own pocket to a group of 42 women making bamboo stools. It was a tiny sum, but it transformed their lives.

They no longer had to borrow from loan sharks at ruinous rates. They could control their own work, their own income, and for the first time, their own futures.

Thus was born the idea of microfinance. The purpose was to provide small loans to the poor without requiring collateral, focused particularly on empowering women. The idea was simple but revolutionary: give people the tools to lift themselves out of poverty.

In 1983, Yunus formally founded the Grameen Bank ("Village Bank") to institutionalize this approach. It operated on principles that flipped traditional banking on its head:

Focus on lending to the poorest.

Trust and community as collateral.

Group lending to build mutual accountability.

It worked. Default rates were astonishingly low. Communities thrived. And a new model of economic empowerment spread like wildfire.

Systemic Change, Not Charity

Like the Romans, who built entire works systems rather than one-off monuments, Yunus was obsessed with creating structures rather than giving handouts.

He did not believe laziness or ignorance was the cause of poverty, but systemic barriers: lack of access to capital, education, and opportunity. Microfinance was going to serve as a long-term viable tool for dismantling the structures that held people back.

Yunus called his vision "social business." These enterprises were designed to solve social problems, not maximize profits. He launched dozens of initiatives beyond banking.

Grameen Telecom: bringing mobile phones to rural Bangladesh, connecting communities to markets and healthcare.

Grameen Shakti: Solar power for off-grid villages.

Grameen Healthcare: affordable clinics for underserved populations.

Each venture was designed *to be self-sustaining*, creating systems that would survive beyond Yunus himself. Yunus was echoing the ancient Roman principle of *durable governance*.

Case Study: Women First

A core tenet of Yunus' model was focusing on *women's empowerment*. Over 90% of Grameen Bank's borrowers were women, based on the observation that women were more likely to reinvest earnings into their families and communities.

The results were transformational:

Higher school attendance rates.

Improved health outcomes.

Reduced child mortality.

Greater social mobility across generations.

In Roman terms, Yunus's building of economic "roads" exhibited the structure and ingenuity to last generations through the *new routes to dignity, health, and opportunity* for families and entire communities to flourish.

Empire of Influence Takeaway:

Think Systemic, Not Sporadic

Yunus did not seek to fix poverty one person at a time. He designed a system that reshaped how the world thinks about lending, business, and the poor.

Bet on People's Potential

Yunus saw resilience and possibility, where others saw risk. Leaders today can learn to see *assets in unlikely places.* Whether it's overlooked talent in an organization or underserved markets, a leader must maintain the awareness of possibilities.

Build Institutions That Outlast You

Grameen Bank and its spin-off ventures have impacted millions, and they continue thriving today. True leadership, like true Roman statecraft, is about leaving structures behind that benefit those who come after. It is much more than just memories.

Global Recognition

For his work, Muhammad Yunus was awarded the Nobel Peace Prize in 2006 (jointly with the Grameen Bank). He has also received the U.S. Presidential Medal of Freedom and the Congressional Gold Medal, along with dozens of other honors.

Perhaps his greatest reward is the living, breathing legacy of economic independence now enjoyed by millions who once lived in extreme poverty.

"Empower One. Uplift Many." is a great theme to live by in this world.

Leading with Integrity in an Uncertain World

Today's leaders face unprecedented challenges. From technological disruption to global crises like climate change and pandemics, leaders must navigate a complex and ever-changing landscape. In this environment, one of the most critical qualities for leaders is *integrity*. Without integrity, even the most talented leaders can lose their way, and their organizations can suffer as a result.

One leader who exemplified integrity in the face of crisis was Frances Oldham Kelsey, the FDA medical officer who refused to approve the drug thalidomide in the U.S. despite immense pressure from pharmaceutical companies. Thalidomide was later found to cause severe birth defects in babies whose mothers had taken the drug during pregnancy. Kelsey's steadfast commitment to *ethical decision-making* saved countless lives and cemented her legacy as a leader of integrity.

For today's entrepreneurs and executives, the lesson is clear: *integrity must guide every decision*. In a world where leaders are often tempted by short-term gains, those who stay true to their principles will build organizations that can withstand even the toughest challenges.

Key Question: Are your decisions guided by integrity, even when the stakes are high? How can you ensure that your leadership is rooted in ethical principles that will stand the test of time?

Case Study III: Merck & Co.—Putting People Over Profits

In the 1980s, Merck & Co., a global pharmaceutical company, faced a profound ethical dilemma. The company had developed a drug called Mectizan, which treated river blindness, a debilitating disease caused by parasitic worms in developing countries. However, the people who needed the drug the most, those in the poorest regions of Africa, could not afford it.

Rather than prioritizing profits, Dr. Roy Vagelos, then CEO of Merck, made the bold decision to give the drug away for free. Merck committed to providing Mectizan to anyone who needed it, for as long as necessary. The decision cost Merck millions of dollars in potential revenue, but it saved millions of lives and positioned Merck as a leader in corporate responsibility.

Today, the Mectizan Donation Program is one of the longest-running global health initiatives, and Merck is celebrated not just for its financial success, but for its commitment to doing what's right.

Empire of Influence Takeaway:

Sometimes doing the right thing means sacrificing profits. Merck's decision to prioritize people over profits shows that ethical leadership can have a profound impact on the world and on the long-term reputation of a company.

As a leader, ask yourself: *Are you willing to make tough decisions that prioritize ethical values over short-term gains?* How can you ensure that your organization's decisions reflect a commitment to doing what's right?

Merck's story is a powerful reminder that *leaders who act with integrity* leave a legacy that extends far beyond the bottom line.

The Future of Leadership: Navigating Uncertainty with Resilience

As we look to the future, one thing is explicitly certain: *uncertainty* will continue to be a defining feature of leadership. Whether it's navigating the ongoing impacts of climate change, managing technological disruption, or responding to global health crises, leaders must be prepared to adapt, innovate, and lead with resilience.

Resilience is about more than just bouncing back from challenges; it also requires *embracing uncertainty* as an opportunity for growth. Leaders who can navigate ambiguity with confidence, flexibility, and optimism will be the ones who succeed in an unpredictable world.

One leader who exemplified resilience in the face of uncertainty is Anne Mulcahy, the former CEO of Xerox. When Mulcahy took over as CEO in 2001, Xerox was on the brink of bankruptcy. The company had been hit hard by the rise of digital technology and faced intense competition from more innovative rivals. Many believed Xerox was doomed.

But Mulcahy refused to give up. She made tough decisions, including cutting jobs and selling off non-core businesses, to stabilize the company. At the same time, she invested in Xerox's core strengths: technology, innovation, and customer service. Her ability to *stay focused on the long-term vision* while managing short-term crises allowed Xerox to recover and eventually thrive once again.

Empire of Influence Takeaway:

Resilience is key to navigating uncertainty. Anne Mulcahy's leadership at Xerox demonstrates that resilience is the key component. It provides the internal fortitude to face challenges head-on and use them as opportunities for transformation.

As a leader, how can you cultivate resilience in yourself and your team? *What strategies can you implement to ensure that your organization thrives in the face of uncertainty?*

Mulcahy's story demonstrates that *resilient leaders do not just survive, they thrive* in the face of adversity.

Special Section for Healthcare Executives:
Leading through Change

Healthcare leaders face some of the most complex and dynamic challenges in any industry. The rapidly changing landscape of healthcare, driven by technological advances, policy shifts, and demographic changes, requires leaders who can *navigate uncertainty with confidence and compassion.* For healthcare executives, leadership must not be solely about managing operations; it must be continually about building systems that prioritize patient care, support healthcare workers, and adapt to future challenges.

Balancing Innovation and Care: Healthcare leaders must embrace innovation while staying focused on the core mission of delivering compassionate care. Whether it's integrating AI into clinical workflows or implementing telemedicine programs, healthcare executives need to balance the promise of new technologies with the needs of patients and healthcare providers.

> *Leadership Tip:* Encourage a culture of innovation that prioritizes patient outcomes. Ensure that new technologies and systems are implemented with a focus on enhancing patient care, not just cutting costs or increasing efficiency.

Supporting Healthcare Workers: The COVID-19 pandemic highlighted the critical importance of supporting healthcare workers. Burnout, stress, and emotional exhaustion are major challenges in the healthcare industry, and leaders must create environments where healthcare workers feel supported, valued, and equipped to provide high-quality care.

> *Leadership Tip:* Implement programs that focus on the mental health and well-being of healthcare workers. This could include offering counseling services, creating

peer support groups, and providing resources for stress management.

Building Resilient Healthcare Systems: Healthcare leaders must also focus on building resilient systems that can adapt to future challenges, whether it's another pandemic, a shift in healthcare policy, or changes in patient demographics. This means investing in infrastructure, technology, and leadership development to ensure that healthcare organizations can thrive in the face of uncertainty.

Leadership Tip: Develop a long-term strategy that prioritizes resilience. Ensure that your healthcare organization is prepared for future challenges by investing in leadership development, technology, and adaptable systems.

Reflection Questions

1. *Building Your Leadership Legacy:*
   What kind of legacy do you want to leave as a leader? Are you focused on immediate successes, or are you building systems and cultures that will endure long after you're gone?

   How can you start making decisions today that will contribute to a lasting leadership legacy? What changes can you make to ensure that your impact goes beyond short-term results?

2. *Leading with Integrity:*
   Think about a recent decision you made as a leader. Did integrity guide your decision-making process? How can

you ensure that ethical principles remain at the heart of your leadership?

Are there areas in your organization where you need to prioritize ethics over profits or short-term gains? How can you build a culture that values integrity and transparency?

3.   *Resilience and Uncertainty:*
How do you handle uncertainty as a leader? Are you resilient in the face of challenges, or do you struggle with ambiguity? What strategies can you implement to build resilience in yourself and your team?

How can you use uncertainty as a catalyst for growth and innovation? What changes can you make in your leadership approach to embrace the unknown with confidence?

4.   *Healthcare Leadership in Change:*
As a healthcare executive, how are you balancing the demand for innovation with the need for compassionate patient care? How can you ensure that new technologies and systems enhance the quality of care?

How are you supporting the well-being of healthcare workers in your organization? What programs or resources can you implement to reduce burnout and stress?

Final Thoughts: Leading the Future

As we conclude this journey through the many facets of leadership, one thing is clear: *the future of leadership is evolving.* Today's leaders must navigate an increasingly complex world, one that demands emotional intelligence, resilience, innovation, and integrity. Whether you're building a business, leading a global corporation, or steering a healthcare organization through change, your ability to adapt, collaborate, and lead with compassion will determine your success.

The future belongs to those who are willing to learn, grow, and embrace new challenges. As a leader, your greatest asset is your ability to inspire others, create lasting systems and cultures, and leave a legacy that reflects your values and vision.

Leadership is not just about what you achieve; it is truly about the impact you have on the people you lead and the world you shape. By leading with integrity, compassion, and resilience, you can build a legacy that endures for generations to come.

Obiter Dictum:

A legacy is not built in a day, and it certainly is not measured in spreadsheets or titles; however, it is something you must shape every day. It is an accumulation of the decisions you have made throughout your life. It cannot be something you just create at the end. I have seen leaders change the course of organizations by aligning their actions with their principles.

The final chapter of leadership is never written in your tenure; it is authored by what endures after you are gone. The systems you established. The people you mentored. The values you instilled in others.

That is how empires are built.

As you close this book and return to your own "empire of influence," ask yourself the one question that defines legacy: *If you walked away today, what would continue to prosper and grow without you?*

The answer…Your legacy in motion.

Scenario:

You have achieved financial success but wonder what will actually remain of your impact.

What Would a Worthy Roman Imperator Do?

Ask yourself: What monuments of meaning am I leaving behind? Wealth fades. Systems, values, and people endure. Lead for eternity, not merely for today.

Having charted the empire of your leadership, the final forum awaits. It's time to reflect, not just on what you have built, but on who you have become. Rome's leaders left echoes. What will yours say?

"Let honor be to you as life, and dishonor as death."

–Sallust

CHAPTER XV

What Will Your Roman Legacy Be?

The Final Forum—Your Legacy Begins Now

Every great leader, from Augustus to Marcus Aurelius, thinks not just about their immediate influence but about the legacy they would leave behind. The concept of a legacy was deeply ingrained in Roman culture; it wasn't enough to simply lead in the moment. Romans sought to create lasting institutions, values, and systems that would endure and benefit future generations. This chapter challenges readers to consider their own impact, asking: "What would your Roman legacy be?" As you reflect on the leadership lessons from ancient Rome, think about how your daily actions, values, and strategies can shape an enduring legacy for the future.

Lessons Learned:

1. Think Long-Term: Roman leaders built structures, systems, and values designed to last for centuries. Today's leaders can focus on creating sustainable growth and lasting impact by thinking beyond immediate gains.

2. Build on Values: Legacy is rooted in values. Romans valued courage, integrity, resilience, and public service. Modern leaders who emphasize these values will leave a legacy that resonates long after they're gone.

3. Empower Future Leaders: Great leaders develop the next generation, creating pathways for future leadership. Like Rome, leaders today can invest in mentorship and resources that empower others.

Legacy Reflections from Roman Leaders

I. Augustus—The Architect of Stability

Background: Augustus spent his entire reign building stability and unity within the Roman Empire, fostering a sense of peace and order. His legacy is one of resilient governance, creating a Rome that would endure long after his death.

Legacy Lesson: Augustus teaches us that a legacy built on stability and unity has lasting power. Leaders today can build systems that withstand challenges by focusing on sustainable growth and cohesion.

Application: Consider what you can put in place to strengthen your organization's foundation, so it remains stable and resilient even after your departure.

II. Marcus Aurelius—The Philosopher King's Ethical Legacy

Background: Known as the "philosopher king," Marcus Aurelius led with integrity, wisdom, and humility, emphasizing Stoic principles in governance. His writings in *Meditations* continue to inspire ethical and self-aware leadership.

Legacy Lesson: Marcus Aurelius reminds us that ethical leadership endures. Leaders who prioritize integrity and personal reflection will leave a legacy of trust and inspiration.

Application: Reflect on how you lead with integrity in daily actions. How can your values shape the culture and reputation of your organization?

III. Cornelia Africana—The Power of Maternal Leadership

Background: Cornelia, mother of the Gracchi brothers, instilled values of duty, integrity, and courage in her sons. Her legacy continued through their reforms, as she shaped future leaders dedicated to Rome's welfare.

Legacy Lesson: Cornelia's life illustrates that legacy can come from empowering others. Leaders who nurture future talent and instill strong values create a ripple effect that impacts generations.

Application: Identify those you can mentor or guide. What values and principles do you want to pass on to those who follow you?

Special Section for Healthcare Executives: Building a Legacy of Compassion and Innovation

Healthcare executives have a unique opportunity to leave a legacy that impacts lives directly. By prioritizing patient-centered care, building strong operational foundations, and fostering a compassionate culture, healthcare leaders can create systems that serve people long after they've moved on. Consider what legacy you want to leave in terms of patient care, team well-being, and community health impact.

Legacy Reflection for Healthcare Leaders

Patient Care: What values guide the care you provide? How can you ensure these values continue within your organization even after you leave?

Sustainability in Healthcare: Like the Roman aqueducts, build systems that ensure resources and care standards are met reliably over time.

Mentoring Future Healthcare Leaders: Encourage the next generation of leaders to adopt a compassionate, patient-centered approach to leadership.

What Would a Worthy Roman Imperator Do?

Crafting Your Legacy of Leadership

Create your "foundation stone": Roman leaders like Augustus and Trajan built lasting infrastructure that future generations would benefit from. Identify a "foundation stone" you can put in place: a program, process, or cultural value that will provide enduring value to your organization.

Develop a personal "Meditations": Marcus Aurelius left behind his *Meditations,* reflections on his values and leadership. Start a personal journal or create written guidelines outlining your values, vision, and insights. Share these reflections with future leaders to pass on your perspective.

Empower a "succession plan": Like Cornelia Africana, who raised future reformers, think about how you can empower future leaders within your organization. Outline a succession plan, invest in mentorship, and identify core leadership qualities you want to see in future leaders.

Profile of Marcus Aurelius—Leading with Lasting Wisdom

Marcus Aurelius: The Philosopher King's Legacy

Core Leadership Lesson: Ethical leadership leaves an enduring legacy.

Insight: Known as the "philosopher king," Marcus Aurelius ruled with wisdom and integrity, recording his reflections in *Meditations.* His ethical approach and emphasis on personal responsibility created a model of principled leadership that remains influential today.

Modern Takeaway: Marcus Aurelius's writings remind us that leadership rooted in integrity inspires trust and admiration. Leaders today can build legacies that last by prioritizing honesty, self-reflection, and a commitment to the greater good.

Key Takeaways from Roman Legacy Building

The leaders of ancient Rome were deeply conscious of their legacies. Whether through infrastructure, values, or mentorship, they understood that their influence could endure for centuries. Today's leaders can draw inspiration from this mindset by prioritizing systems, values, and mentorship that build lasting impact.

Think Long-Term: True legacies are built through sustainable systems and resilient foundations.

Define Your Values: A legacy is defined by values. Decide on the principles that will guide your decisions and the culture you create.

Empower the Next Generation: Mentorship and talent development ensure that your values and vision continue, building an organization that thrives well into the future.

Reflection Questions

1. *What values do you want to define your leadership?*
    Write down three core values that you would like others
    to remember about your leadership.

2. *What systems or practices have you put in place to
    ensure lasting impact?*
    Think of one area where you can implement sustainable
    processes, policies, or programs that could endure.

3. *Who are you empowering to carry on your vision?*
    Consider how you can actively mentor or support
    emerging leaders who will continue your legacy.

Final Call to Action: Building Your Own Roman Legacy

As you reflect on the lessons from ancient Rome, think deeply
about the impact you want to leave behind. Whether in business,
healthcare, education, or community leadership, your actions
today shape the legacy of tomorrow. By building lasting structures,
fostering inclusive cultures, and investing in future leaders, you can
create a legacy that echoes through the lives of those you touch.

Remember, Rome wasn't built in a day; however, it was built
to last. Lead with vision, integrity, and resilience, and consider
every decision as part of a greater legacy. As you look back on the
timeless lessons of Rome, ask yourself:

What will my Roman legacy be?

I have provided these Latin terms, alongside their modern
business equivalents, to offer a deeper understanding of Roman
leadership values and how they relate to today's leadership

challenges. My hope is that by adding an authentic Roman touch, we can connect more meaningfully with the timeless aspects of impactful leadership.

Obiter Dictum:

If this book has encouraged you to think differently, then I've done my job. This book is the result of a lifetime of lessons. Lessons which have been hard-earned and others gratefully received. I believe our lives, like Rome's architecture, are measured by what we build and by how long it endures.

In healthcare leadership, I have seen firsthand how the smallest decisions have an incredible impact. How you treat a colleague, how you handle pressure, how you champion or ignore a broken process, can echo long after you are gone. Like Rome's aqueducts, the invisible infrastructure you lay down today determines whether the organization thrives tomorrow.

So ask yourself each day: *Am I building for applause or endurance?* In the end, applause fades; but, resilient systems, empowered teams, and a culture rooted in clarity: That is what lives on.

APPENDIX

"Valor grows by daring, fear by holding back."

Tacitus

GLOSSARY OF KEY ROMAN TERMS
FOR MODERN LEADERS

Auctoritas

Definition: Authority and influence, often informal but respected.

Business Translation: A leader's *credibility and influence* within an organization, earned through expertise, trust, and the respect of others.

Example: A CEO with auctoritas is not just a titleholder but someone whose decisions and actions command respect and inspire others to follow

Clementia

Definition: Mercy, leniency, and compassion shown by leaders, particularly in victory.

Business Translation: *Empathy and kindness* in leadership, especially in interactions with teams and employees.

Example: A leader displaying clementia might show patience during challenging times and support team members facing personal struggles, recognizing the value of compassionate leadership.

Consilium

Definition: Counsel or wisdom, often used to refer to advisory bodies in Roman governance.

Business Translation: *Strategic guidance and advisory input,* particularly in decision-making contexts.

Example: Leaders with a strong consilium surround themselves with trusted advisors, ensuring they receive balanced and well-informed perspectives.

Dignitas

Definition: A sense of personal honor, dignity, and reputation earned through contributions to society.

Business Translation: *Reputation and respect* within an industry, based on credibility and accomplishments.

Example: A leader with dignitas has built a solid professional reputation that earns respect from colleagues, employees, and competitors alike.

Disciplina

Definition: The Roman concept of discipline, self-control, and commitment to continuous improvement.

Business Translation: *Professional discipline and development*, with a commitment to learning, growth, and consistent performance.

Example: Leaders who practice disciplina focus on skill development, setting high standards for themselves and their teams.

Fides

Definition: Trustworthiness and reliability, particularly in relationships and obligations.

Business Translation: *Trust and integrity*—the foundation of strong partnerships, team morale, and customer loyalty.

Example: Leaders who embody fides keep promises, foster trust, and demonstrate dependability, strengthening organizational cohesion and stakeholder confidence.

Fortitudo

Definition: Courage and resilience in the face of adversity.

Business Translation: *Resilience and determination* in leadership, essential during challenging times.

Example: Leaders who exhibit fortitudo stay focused on their goals even during setbacks, inspiring their teams to persevere.

Gloria

Definition: Glory, honor, and public recognition of one's achievements.

Business Translation: *Professional success and recognition*—the pursuit of accomplishments that bring pride and respect to an organization.

Example: Leaders driven by gloria seek to achieve results that elevate their teams and organizations, celebrating achievements that bring collective pride.

Gravitas

Definition: A sense of seriousness, dignity, and responsibility expected in leadership roles.

Business Translation: *Professionalism and composure*, especially in high-pressure situations.

Example: Gravitas in business leadership means maintaining calm, rational decision-making and presenting oneself as a stable, confident authority figure.

Imperator

Definition: A commander granted authority after a major victory; later, the title for Rome's supreme leader.

Business Translation: A *decisive leader* who takes charge during pivotal moments and drives the organization toward meaningful wins.

Example: An individual who steps forward when a company faces its biggest challenge yet, is an imperator: steady, strategic and ready to lead.

Imperium

Definition: Supreme executive power granted to Roman leaders, especially in military or administrative roles.

Business Translation: *Executive authority* within a company or organization, particularly in high-stakes situations or decisions.

Example: A founder or executive exercising imperium makes critical decisions impacting the direction and success of the organization, much like a Roman empire's military or governmental leader.

Libertas

Definition: Freedom and autonomy, a valued aspect of Roman citizenship.

Business Translation: *Empowerment and autonomy* within an organization, allowing team members to make decisions and innovate.

Example: Leaders who promote libertas create a work environment that values individual autonomy, encouraging employees to take initiative and drive change.

Militia

Definition: The military service and duty expected of Roman citizens, emphasizing structure and unity.

Business Translation: Organizational discipline and structure, where each team member has a clearly defined role and responsibility.

Example: Leaders who value militia create a strong sense of structure and purpose, unifying their teams and ensuring each person understands their contribution to the organization's goals.

Pax Romana

Definition: The Roman Peace, a period of stability and prosperity across the empire.

Business Translation: *Organizational harmony and stability,* fostering a productive, peaceful work environment.

Example: A leader who creates pax in the organization builds a culture of collaboration and peace, where employees feel safe, valued, and productive.

Pietas

Definition: Duty, loyalty, and respect toward the gods, family, and Rome.

Business Translation: *Dedication and loyalty* to one's organization, mission, and core values.

Example: Leaders with pietas demonstrate a deep commitment to their organization's values and purpose, inspiring similar loyalty among team members.

Res Publica

Definition: The Roman term for the "public affair" or the state; the welfare of society.

Business Translation: *Organizational mission and public responsibility*, focusing on the broader impact beyond profits.

Example: Leaders focused on res publica prioritize a mission that benefits society and positions the organization as a force for good in the community.

Salus

Definition: Health, safety, and the well-being of society.

Business Translation: *Corporate Social Responsibility* (CSR) and prioritizing the well-being of employees and communities.

Example: Leaders focused on salus ensure their organization promotes wellness, safety, and creates a positive impact on society, aligning their goals with social responsibility.

Senatus

Definition: The Senate, Rome's advisory and legislative body, representing diverse perspectives.

Business Translation: *Board of advisors or executive team*, providing leadership with diverse insights and guidance.

Example: A leader's senatus could include trusted advisors or board members who offer feedback and help shape the organization's strategic direction.

Virtus

Definition: Valor, courage, and excellence, often associated with moral integrity.

Business Translation: *Character and integrity*—the core values that define a leader's strength and ethical foundation.

Example: Leaders with virtus show moral integrity, particularly in difficult times, setting a strong ethical standard for the organization.

EXPANDED TABLE OF CONTENTS

Introduction
Why Rome? Why Now?

The Timeless Impact of Leadership

- Overview of the relevance of ancient Roman leadership principles today.
- How the lessons of Rome can inform modern executive success.
- *Gladiator*—A Review in the Arena

Part I—The Foundations of Leadership

Chapter I—The Empire Within
Mastery before Mission

Focus: The internal foundation of leadership is self-awareness, discipline, and personal integrity. True empire-building starts within.

- Understanding the importance of preparation, finding your way, and leading with purpose to positively impact the organization.
- Key lessons from ancient leaders applied to building modern businesses, focused on building customer and patient-centered systems.
- *Special Section for Healthcare Executives:* Developing future leaders and addressing complex healthcare challenges.
- Reflection Questions

Chapter II—Eyes on Eternity

Augustus and the Architecture of Vision

Focus: Visionary leadership means building for generations, not just quarterly wins. This chapter explores how long-term thinking forges empires that outlast their creators.

- Visionary leadership inspired by figures like Julius Caesar, offering lessons on anticipating future needs and long-term planning.
- How bold visionaries in business and healthcare shape the future by challenging norms.
- Special Section for Healthcare Executives: The importance of strategic vision in building healthcare systems.
- Reflection Questions

Chapter III—Rebels with a Cause

Disrupting Like a Roman General

Focus: Innovation often means challenging convention. This chapter highlights the courage required to break molds, defy norms, and reshape systems.

- Trajan's strategic growth and disruption as a model for innovators.
- Case studies on modern disruptors in healthcare and business, emphasizing the value of challenging the status quo.
- Special Section for Healthcare Executives: Fostering innovation in healthcare to improve patient outcomes.
- Reflection Questions

Chapter IV—The Moral Standard
Integrity from Forum to Boardroom

Focus: Ethical leadership builds trust, resilience, and legacy. In Rome and today, moral courage separates the powerful from the principled.

- Ethical leadership principles drawn from Cicero and Antoninus Pius, emphasizing the importance of justice and integrity.
- Lessons on making morally sound decisions and leading with integrity in healthcare and business.
- Special Section for Healthcare Executives: Navigating ethical dilemmas in patient care and healthcare leadership.
- Reflection Questions

Chapter V—Holding the Line
Fortitude at the Frontiers

Focus: Strategic leadership emerges in times of crisis. This chapter explores the strength of stabilizing forces and the wisdom of timely restraint.

- Strategic crisis management inspired by Hadrian, focusing on prevention and preparedness.
- Modern examples of leaders who have navigated crises with resilience and adaptability.
- Special Section for Healthcare Executives: Leading through crises in healthcare, with a focus on foresight and planning.
- Reflection Questions

Part II—The Practice of Influence

Chapter VI—Strength in Service

Humility in the Age of Empire

Focus: Servant leadership isn't soft; it's foundational. From ancient Rome to the modern boardroom, true influence is built through lifting others.

- The servant leadership model exemplified by Cincinnatus, highlighting humility and a focus on service.
- Modern case studies in compassionate leadership, showing how humility builds stronger teams and loyal followers.
- Special Section for Healthcare Executives: Benefits of servant leadership in healthcare, improving staff morale and patient care.
- Reflection Questions

Chapter VII—Builders of the Future

Trajan's Blueprint for Legacy

Focus: Transformational leaders do not merely fix problems—they build resilient systems. This chapter explores scalable models and lasting design.

- Augustus' vision for a stable empire as a model for creating enduring systems.
- Lessons from modern transformational leaders who have focused on building sustainable organizations.
- Special Section for Healthcare Executives: Developing resilient healthcare systems for long-term sustainability.
- Reflection Questions

Chapter VIII—One Empire, Many Voices

Senate, Legions, and the Power of Collaboration

Focus: Empires rise when many work as one. This chapter explores the strategic power of shared vision and collective leadership.

- Collaborative leadership and unity, drawing lessons from Antoninus Pius and the Roman legions.
- How teamwork and shared vision can drive innovation and organizational success.
- Special Section for Healthcare Executives: The role of interdisciplinary collaboration in healthcare.
- Reflection Questions

Chapter IX—Healing with Honor

Compassion as a Leadership Imperative

Focus: Empathy is not a luxury; it is a leadership essential. This chapter reveals how emotional intelligence shapes lives, teams, and entire systems.

- Compassionate leadership through the example of Dame Cicely Saunders, founder of the hospice movement.
- Lessons on the power of empathy and emotional intelligence in transforming healthcare and business environments.
- Special Section for Healthcare Executives: Integrating compassion into healthcare for holistic, patient-centered care.
- Reflection Questions

Chapter X—Beyond the Marble

The Silent Might of Roman Women

Focus: The unseen often outlasts the visible. This chapter uncovers the impact of Roman women and the lessons they offer in subtle, strategic, and sustained influence.

- Influential leadership without a formal title, as exhibited by Livia Drusilla, Agrippina the Younger, Cornelia Africana, and Julia Domna.
- Lessons on the power of trust, building strategic alliances, adaptability, and the importance of intellectual necessity in

healthcare and business environments.
- Special Section for Healthcare Executives: Enhancing leadership influence to further support the mission of caring for the patients and community.
- Reflection Questions

Part III—Systems, Strategy, and Legacy

Chapter XI—Thrones and Forums
Balancing Governance and Influence

Focus: Leadership thrives when power is shared with wisdom. This chapter explores the tension and harmony between decisive authority and collaborative governance.

- The strongest leaders know when to rule and when to listen—effective governance thrives on balancing authority with collaboration.
- Rome's durability came from blending decisive emperors with the deliberative Senate—today's leadership should follow this model of shared power and decision-making.
- Special Section for Healthcare Executives: Balancing C-suite decision-making with medical staff input by building forums such as cross-disciplinary committees, executive advisory teams, and ethics boards to promote trust, avoid burnout, and empower better healthcare decisions.
- Reflection Questions

Chapter XII—The Infrastructure of Greatness
Aqueducts, Roads, and Strategic Systems

Focus: Greatness is engineered from the ground up. This chapter explores how systems thinking, resiliency, and thoughtful design form the backbone of enduring leadership.

- Rome's most enduring legacy was not in monuments, it was in the systems. The need for smart leaders to invest in operations that scale and adapt.
- True infrastructure is often invisible until it fails. Why it's essential to build systems today that your successors will thank you for in the future.
- Special Section for Healthcare Executives: From electronic health records to emergency response workflows, the infrastructure behind care delivery must be intentionally focused on a healing environment, not hindering care.
- Reflection Questions

Chapter XIII—The Cultivated Mind
Lifelong Learning, Intellectual Discipline, and the Roman Art of Reflection

Focus: Wisdom, like Rome, is built over time. This chapter examines how intellectual curiosity and philosophical reflection elevate decision-making, develop wisdom, and strengthen as well as anchor enduring leadership.

- Why leaders who invest in their intellectual growth outperform those who rely only on instinct or experience alone.
- Like a Roman philosopher-statesman, modern leaders must cultivate daily disciplines of thought, reflection, and learning.
- Special Section for Healthcare Executives: The importance of healthcare leaders staying current with medical innovation, policy shifts, and positive ethical evolution. Intellectual humility is your most valuable credential and to never stop learning.
- Reflection Questions

Chapter XIV—*Legacy in Motion*

How to Build Influence That Lasts Beyond You

Focus: Building a Leadership Empire that Endures

- The fact that every leader leaves a legacy—the question is whether it will be intentional, meaningful, and lasting.
- Like Rome, why your leadership must be designed with structure, purpose, and values that can outlive your direct control.
- Special Section for Healthcare Executives: Your decisions shape the culture of care, the systems that remain, and the leadership pipelines you leave behind. What you build today will become the inheritance of future patients and professionals.
- Reflection Questions

Chapter XV: *What Will Your Roman Legacy Be?*

The Final Forum—Your Legacy Begins Now

- The true measure of influence is not what you achieve, but what you empower others to become.
- Your Roman legacy is not written in stone, it is forged daily in decisions, values, and the people you uplift.
- Special Section for Healthcare Executives: In medicine, legacies are human. What you teach, how you lead, and how you listen may shape generations of caregivers and patients long after your final day in the organization.
- Reflection Questions

RECOMMENDED READING

Confronting the Classics: Traditions, Adventures, and Innovations
Mary Beard

Emperor of Rome
Mary Beard

The Roman Triumph
Mary Beard

The Portable Roman Reader
edited by Basil Davenport

The Roads to Rome: A History of Imperial Expansion
Catherine Fletcher

In the Name of Rome: The Men Who Won the Roman Empire
Adrian Goldsworthy

Roman Warfare
Adrian Goldsworthy

The Roman Way
Edith Hamilton

Lives of the Caesars
Suetonius, translated by Tom Holland

The Thoughts of the Emperor Marcus Aurelius Antoninus
translated by George Long, illustrated by W. Russell Flint

The Way of the Gladiator
Daniel P. Mannix

*The Quest for Character: What the Story of Socrates and Alcibiades
Teaches Us about Our Search for Good Leaders*
Massimo Pigliucci

The Landmark Julius Caesar
edited by Kurt A. Raaflaub; series editor Robert B. Strassler

The Stoics Illustrated: Ancient Wisdom for Modern Living
Paul Scade

Ten Caesars: Roman Emperors from Augustus to Constantine
Barry Strauss

The Romans: A 2,000-Year History
Edward J. Watts

Wisdom Takes Work
Ryan Holliday

ACKNOWLEDGEMENTS

I wish to convey my sincere appreciation to all individuals who contributed to the development and completion of this book. Foremost, I extend my deepest gratitude to my family for their steadfast support and encouragement throughout every stage of this project. My wife's continual support proved invaluable during both research and writing, while our daughters, Chantelle and Sheridan, offered insightful feedback and meticulous editing over several years.

I would also like to thank my friends and colleagues, whose constructive feedback and thoughtful discussions significantly influenced the direction of this work. Special recognition goes to Jim Galvin and Mary Ann Lackland at Tenth Power Publishing, whose editorial expertise and commitment were crucial in refining each chapter and overseeing the production process. My sincere thanks to Mary Gardner for her thoughtful advice and counsel. I would like to acknowledge the very talented Reese Reider for his artistic illustrations. His creativity is impressive, and I believe he has a very promising career ahead.

Additionally, I am grateful to the numerous scholars, writers, and specialists in Roman history and business whose published resources underpinned much of this work. Many of these contributors are acknowledged in the Further Reading section. While their input has been indispensable, any remaining errors are entirely my own responsibility.

Finally, I appreciate the continued enthusiasm and guidance of my readers and mentors, whose support inspired me to carry this project to completion. Without the contributions and encouragement of these remarkable individuals, this book would not have been possible. Thank you all for your integral roles in this journey.

For more purchasing options and information on the book,
visit the publisher at www.tenthpowerpublishing.com.

For more information about the author,
visit www.RodneyDReider.com.